URBAN BIRD

# THE JOY OF ORIGAMI

ELEPHANT
IN PAJAMAS

## *by* MARGARET VAN SICKLEN

PAPER DOLLHOUSE

WORKMAN PUBLISHING · NEW YORK

*To my parents, Peggy and Doug Van Sicklen, for encouraging my curious mind. And to Sven Nebelung, my turtle dove, for all his love and support.*

AUTHOR'S ACKNOWLEDGMENTS: *The Joy of Origami* combines traditional and original models. I am indebted to many origamists the world over who have kindly contributed their models—particularly to Laura Kruskal, Anita Barbour, Francis Ow, Kunihiko Kasahara, and the fabulous Florence Temko.

Very special thanks to Barbie Altorfer for flexing her creative muscle and pulling this book together.

Library of Congress Cataloging-in-Publication Data is available.

ISBN-13: 978-0-7611-3988-1

Workman books are available at special discounts when purchased in bulk for premiums and sales promotions as well as for fund-raising or educational use. Special editions or book excerpts can also be created to specification. For details, contact the Special Sales Director at the address below:

Workman Publishing Company, Inc.
225 Varick Street
New York, NY 10014-4381
www.workman.com

First Printing October 2005

10 9 8 7

# TABLE OF CONTENTS

# THE SHIP OF 1,000 CRANES STARTS WITH A SINGLE FOLD. . . .

Origami starts with a piece of paper and a curious mind. I was born with a curious mind, but it took me a few years to find the paper. One day, as an adult, while roaming the halls of the American Museum of Natural History in New York, I came across an Origami USA class. An instructor was teaching a group of 8-year-olds the Jumping Frog. I couldn't help but join in the fun. Within moments, I completed my very own Jumping Frog and, boy, was it cute (and an excellent jumper).

Ever since that day, origami has played a role in my life. In 1998, I had the idea for a daily origami calendar (now published by Workman Publishing as the ORIGAMI PAGE-A-DAY®). As I've heard via hundreds of letters and e-mail, it's great to spend a few moments every day folding a model. So many folks have told me how much fun it is to share their creations with coworkers, family, and friends.

This, to me, is the joy of origami. It's folding for a friend or even a stranger. The joy of origami is in the "wow!," "that's cool!," and the feeling of accomplishment. It's in the smile of a tough cab driver after I handed him a dollar bill folded as a rabbit. It's in the wide-eyed disbelief of a whiny kid for whom I made a Flapping Bird. It's in the rapt attention with which a class of tough inner-city kids sat folding an Urban Bird.

So dive in. Let's spread the joy of origami together.

## HELPFUL HINTS

1. Fold on a flat surface.
2. Review all the diagrams before folding a model.
3. Check the next step as you are folding to see where you're heading.
4. Take it easy and have fun folding! Origami is a brainteaser. Very few people "get it" on the first try. Like any skill, folding will come to you when the moves become automatic.

# ORIGAMI SYMBOLS

These diagrams, used throughout this book, are the origami ABCs. Practice the folds on the first sheet in the origami paper section.

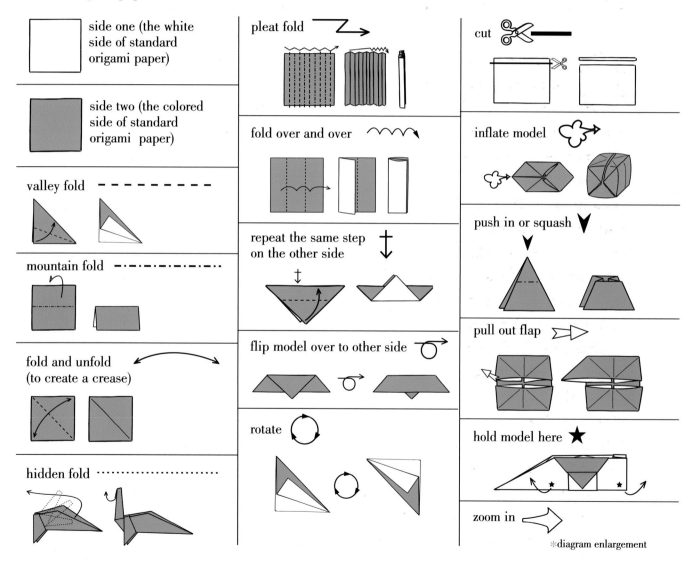

side one (the white side of standard origami paper)

side two (the colored side of standard origami paper)

valley fold

mountain fold

fold and unfold (to create a crease)

hidden fold

pleat fold

fold over and over

repeat the same step on the other side

flip model over to other side

rotate

cut

inflate model

push in or squash

pull out flap

hold model here

zoom in

*diagram enlargement

# ORIGAMI BASICS

The squash is a common origami maneuver.

## squash

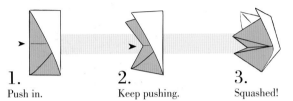

**1.** Push in.

**2.** Keep pushing.

**3.** Squashed!

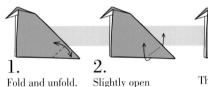

*Try the reverse folds on the practice sheet provided in the origami paper section after page 152.

---

The inside and outside reverse folds are two common folds.

## inside reverse fold

**1.** Fold and unfold.

**2.** Slightly open model and fold flap to the inside.

Wow, a wonderful bird's head!

## outside reverse fold

**1.** Fold and unfold.

**2.** Slightly open flap and fold to the outside of the model.

The opposite of inside reverse fold.

A super cute tail!

---

Bases are the building blocks of origami models.

## blintz base

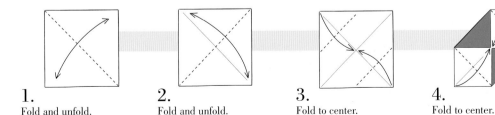

**1.** Fold and unfold.

**2.** Fold and unfold.

**3.** Fold to center.

**4.** Fold to center.

**5.**

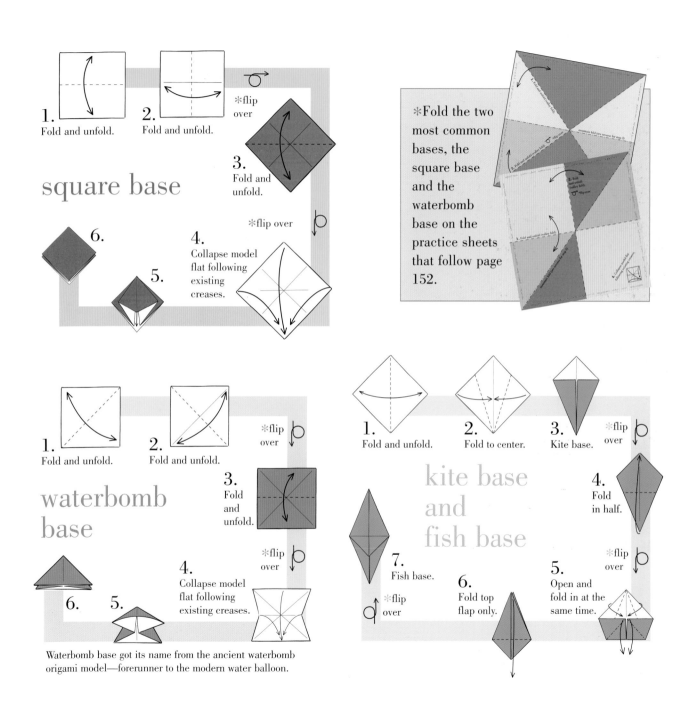

**1.** Fold and unfold.

**2.** Fold and unfold.

*flip over

**3.** Fold and unfold.

*flip over

## square base

**6.**

**5.**

**4.** Collapse model flat following existing creases.

*Fold the two most common bases, the square base and the waterbomb base on the practice sheets that follow page 152.

**1.** Fold and unfold.

**2.** Fold and unfold.

*flip over

## waterbomb base

**3.** Fold and unfold.

*flip over

**6.**

**5.**

**4.** Collapse model flat following existing creases.

Waterbomb base got its name from the ancient waterbomb origami model—forerunner to the modern water balloon.

**1.** Fold and unfold.

**2.** Fold to center.

**3.** Kite base.

*flip over

## kite base and fish base

**4.** Fold in half.

**7.** Fish base.

*flip over

**6.** Fold top flap only.

**5.** Open and fold in at the same time.

*flip over

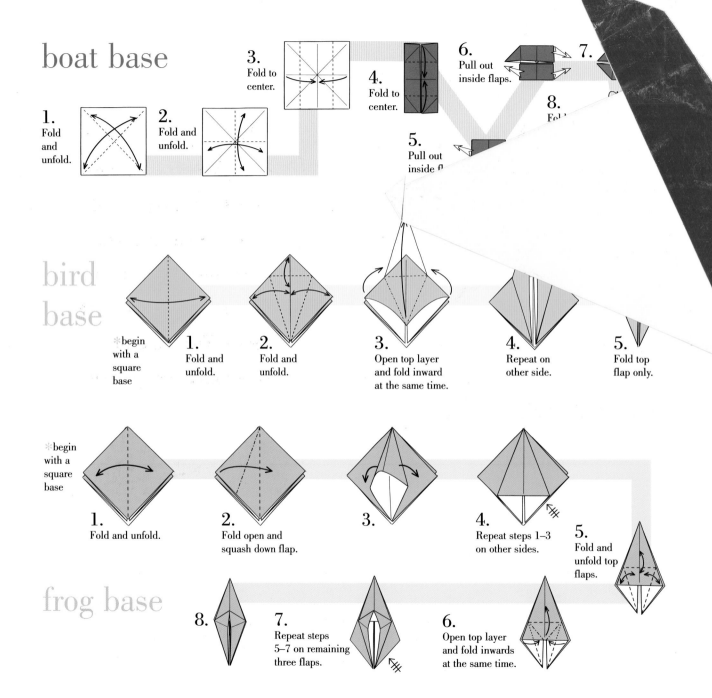

# boat base

**1.** Fold and unfold.

**2.** Fold and unfold.

**3.** Fold to center.

**4.** Fold to center.

**5.** Pull out inside fl

**6.** Pull out inside flaps.

**7.**

**8.** Fol

# bird base

※begin with a square base

**1.** Fold and unfold.

**2.** Fold and unfold.

**3.** Open top layer and fold inward at the same time.

**4.** Repeat on other side.

**5.** Fold top flap only.

※begin with a square base

**1.** Fold and unfold.

**2.** Fold open and squash down flap.

**3.**

**4.** Repeat steps 1–3 on other sides.

**5.** Fold and unfold top flaps.

# frog base

**8.**

**7.** Repeat steps 5–7 on remaining three flaps.

**6.** Open top layer and fold inwards at the same time.

# ladybug

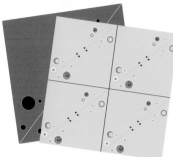

*Recommended paper*

*Cut the paper with the small bugs into quarters to fold a family.*

As a California girl, I've always had a special feeling for ladybugs. They hold a revered place in my state's history for saving our citrus groves from orange- and lemon-sucking insect pests (plus, they're darn cute). The origami Ladybug is ideal for beginners because it has only a few simple steps and completing it will build one's all-important folding confidence. There are two choices of paper: go traditional with black and red or join me in paying tribute to the California orange.

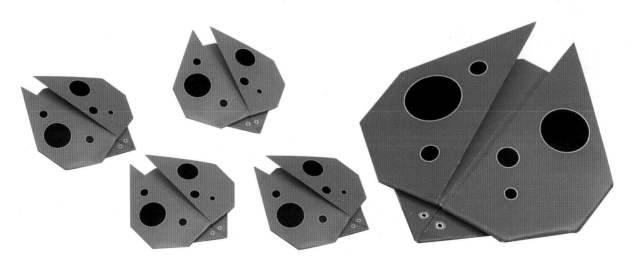

# HOW TO FOLD THE LADYBUG

◆◇◇◇ LEVEL OF DIFFICULTY

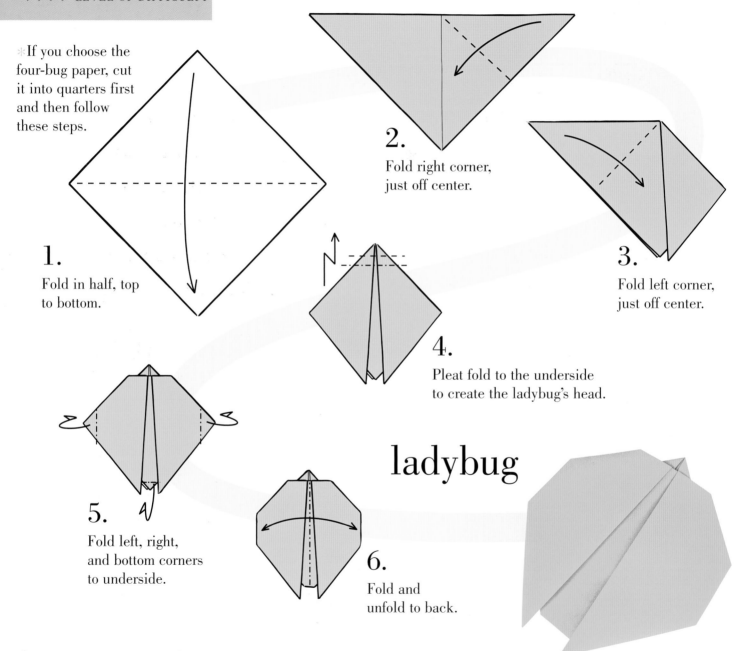

＊If you choose the four-bug paper, cut it into quarters first and then follow these steps.

**1.**

Fold in half, top to bottom.

**2.**

Fold right corner, just off center.

**3.**

Fold left corner, just off center.

**4.**

Pleat fold to the underside to create the ladybug's head.

ladybug

**5.**

Fold left, right, and bottom corners to underside.

**6.**

Fold and unfold to back.

# butterfly

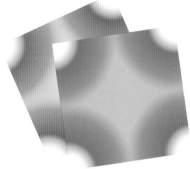

*Recommended paper*

This model was designed by Michael LaFosse as a gift for an eminent entomologist, Alice Gray, of the American Museum of Natural History. Dr. Gray was more than just a leading bug authority. Along with Lillian Oppenheimer, she was one of the great pioneers of origami in the United States. There have been many origami butterfly models; after all, they're just about everyone's favorite insect. But Michael's design is my all-time favorite. Pin it on a t-shirt and you have the perfect fashion accessory for summer.

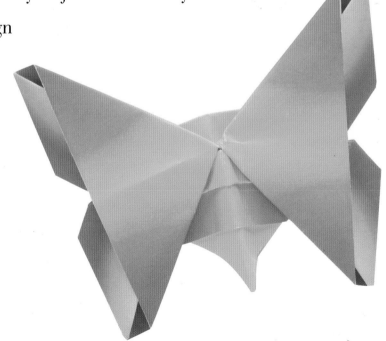

# How to fold the Butterfly

◆◆◆◇ LEVEL OF DIFFICULTY

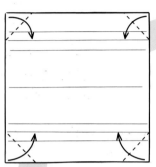

## 5.
Fold all four corners to the creases made in step 4.

## 6.
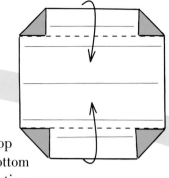

Fold top and bottom on existing creases.

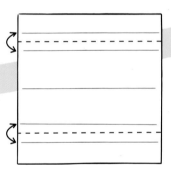

## 4.
Fold and unfold.

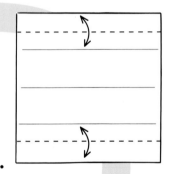

## 3.
Fold and unfold.

## 1.
Fold and unfold.

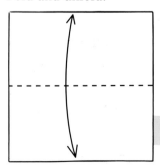

## 2.
Fold and unfold to center crease.

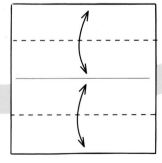

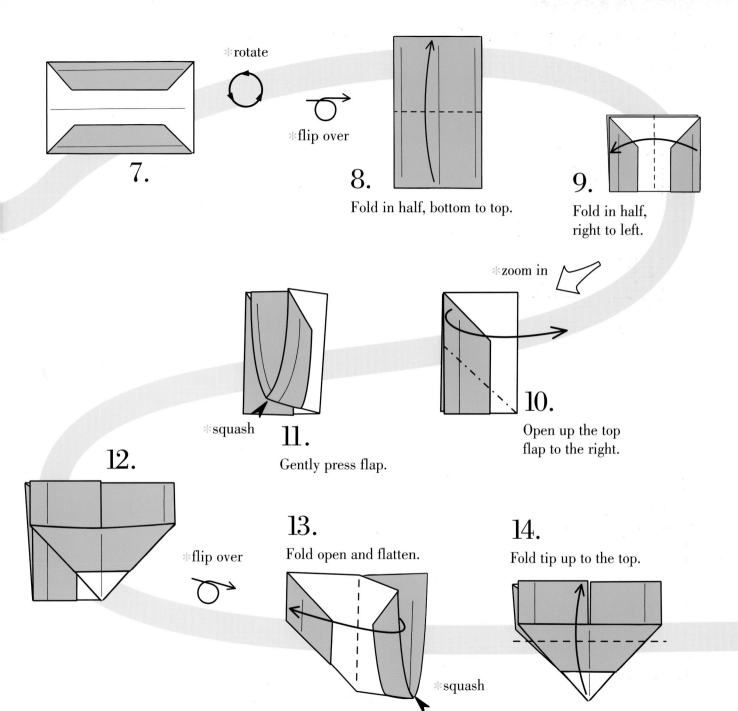

7.

*rotate

*flip over

8.

Fold in half, bottom to top.

9.

Fold in half,
right to left.

*zoom in

*squash 11.

Gently press flap.

10.

Open up the top
flap to the right.

12.

*flip over

13.

Fold open and flatten.

*squash

14.

Fold tip up to the top.

## 19.

Fold left edge to the right. Keeping your finger on it, fold bottom wing to the left and crease.

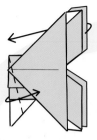

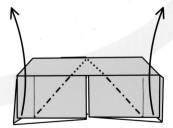

## butterfly

for Alice Gray,
by Michael LaFosse

## 18.

Fold in half, left flap behind right flap.

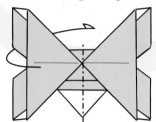

*squash

## 17.

Gently press down.

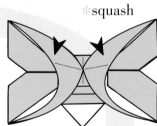

## 15.

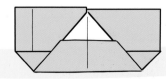

*flip over

*rotate

## 16.

Open up and flatten both wings.

# floating lotus

The lotus is a magical flower. Observe one in a pond and it seems to have actually taken root on the surface of the water. The origami model inspired by the lotus is magical too—it floats, and here's how. Fold the flower and then rub a thick layer of wax on the underside of the model (use a crayon or a candle—experiment with plain paper first!). Then lightly place the flower in a bowl of water. It should float for hours and delight your eye—and your friends and family.

*Recommended paper*

# HOW TO FOLD THE FLOATING LOTUS

◆◆◇◇ LEVEL OF DIFFICULTY

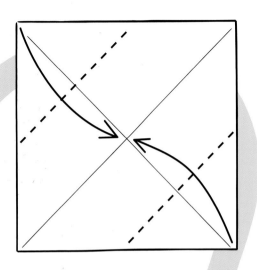

**2.**

Fold two corners to the center.

**4.**

Look! You've made a blintz base.

**1.**

Fold and unfold.

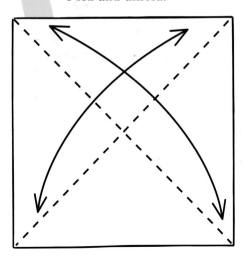

**3.**

Fold other two corners to the center.

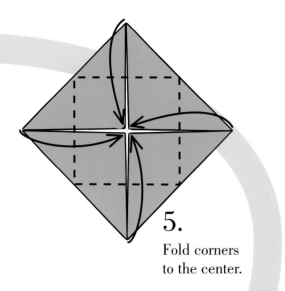

**5.**

Fold corners
to the center.

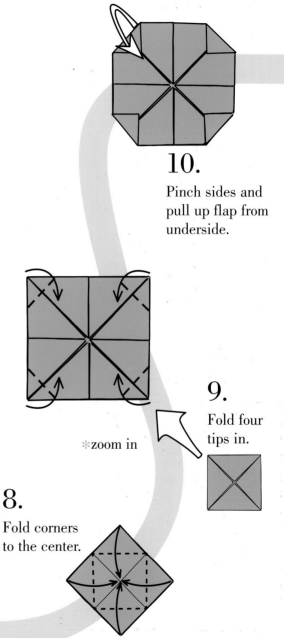

**10.**

Pinch sides and
pull up flap from
underside.

**6.**

Fold corners
to the center.

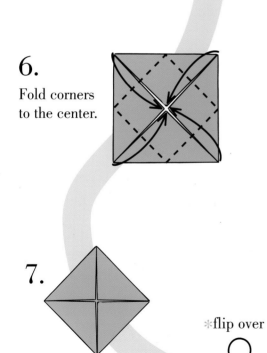

**9.**

Fold four
tips in.

*zoom in

**8.**

Fold corners
to the center.

**7.**

*flip over

## 11.

Repeat on the other three flaps.

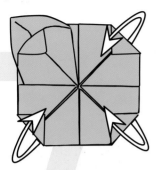

*repeat

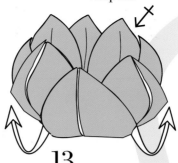

## 13.

Gently pull out all remaining flaps from the underside. Repeat on the other side.

## 14.

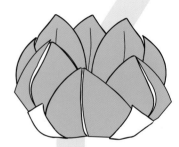

*flip over

## 12.

## 15.

Rub a thick layer of wax (using a crayon or a candle) on the underside of the model to make it float longer.

# floating lotus

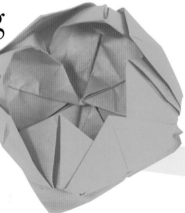

*flip over

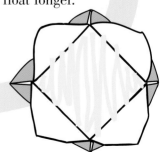

# inflatable tulip

Paper flowers are always in season. Brighten up any room by folding a bouquet of these colorful beauties (the paper for the flower was inspired by Tiffany glass). Inflating the flower is a fun twist at the end, but the best part of making this model is when you gently peel back the petals to give them a jaunty shape. Then set them on their stems (see page 14) and find a suitable vase for your creation.

*Recommended paper for flower and stems*

# How to fold the Inflatable Tulip

◆◆◇◇ LEVEL OF DIFFICULTY

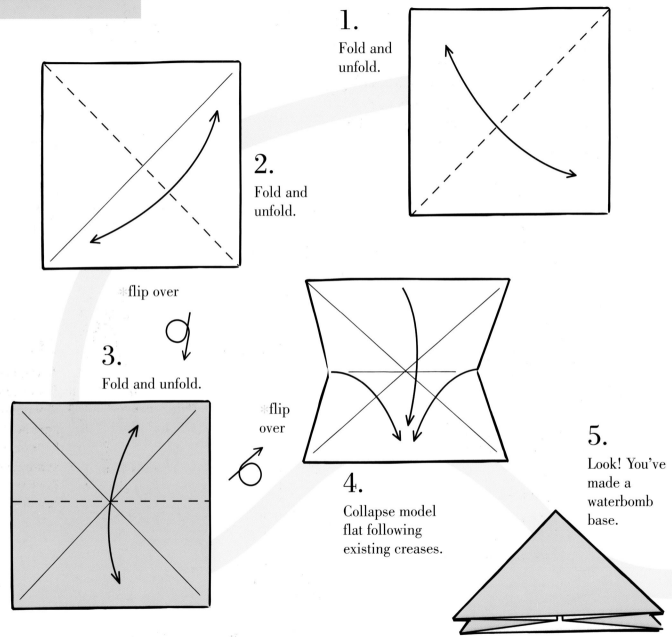

**1.** Fold and unfold.

**2.** Fold and unfold.

*flip over

**3.** Fold and unfold.

*flip over

**4.** Collapse model flat following existing creases.

**5.** Look! You've made a waterbomb base.

# inflatable tulip

**8.**
Fold left corner of top layer over to the right, a little past the center.

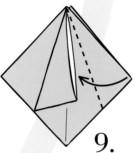

**7.**
Fold top left flap over to the right. Repeat on other side.

*repeat

**9.**
Fold and tuck right corner of top layer into the previous fold.

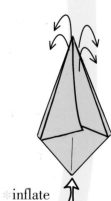

**11.**
Now make the flower bloom. Blow into the hole at the bottom, and gently peel back the four petals.

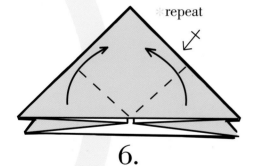

**6.**
Fold left and right corners of top layer in toward center. Repeat on other side.

*repeat

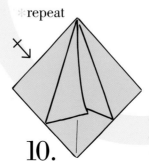

*repeat

*inflate

**10.**
Repeat steps 8 and 9 on other side.

# How to fold the Stems

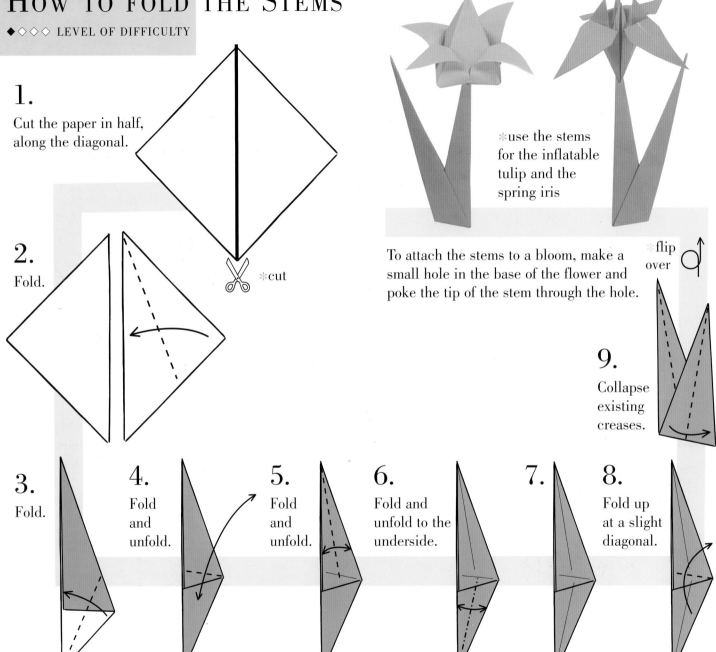

**1.** Cut the paper in half, along the diagonal.

*cut

*use the stems for the inflatable tulip and the spring iris

To attach the stems to a bloom, make a small hole in the base of the flower and poke the tip of the stem through the hole.

*flip over

**2.** Fold.

**9.** Collapse existing creases.

**3.** Fold.

**4.** Fold and unfold.

**5.** Fold and unfold.

**6.** Fold and unfold to the underside.

**7.**

**8.** Fold up at a slight diagonal.

# spring iris

Ready for a challenge? Look no further. This model is one of the most complicated in the book. When you fold our Spring Iris for the first time,

you may feel the chill of winter as you break into a cold sweat. Steady on, my fellow folder! By the final maneuver of this delightful model, you will feel the sweet warmth of spring. And what could be a better feeling, I ask you? Try it!

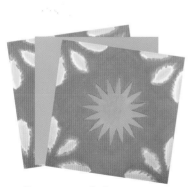

*Recommended paper for flower and stems*

# How to fold the Spring Iris

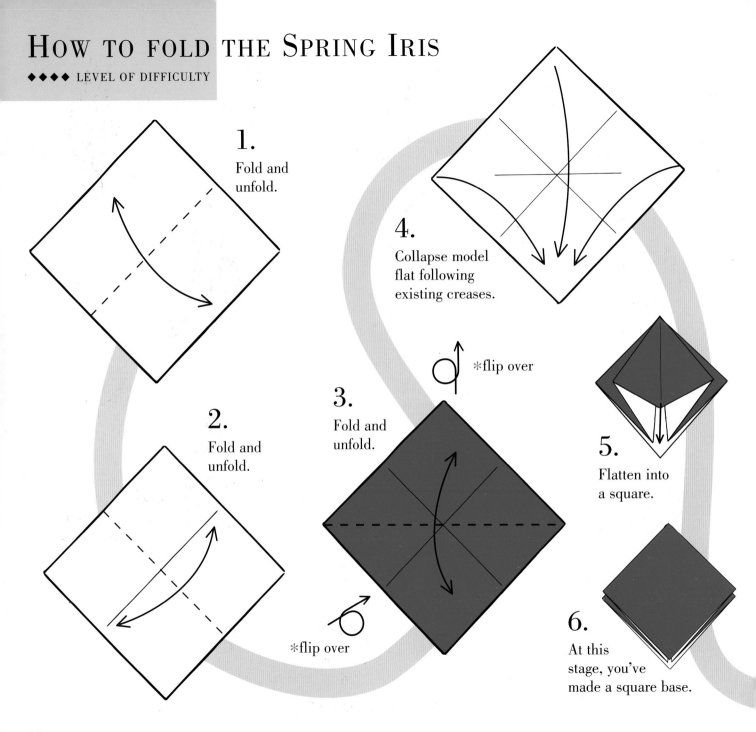

**1.** Fold and unfold.

**2.** Fold and unfold.

**3.** Fold and unfold.

*flip over

**4.** Collapse model flat following existing creases.

*flip over

**5.** Flatten into a square.

**6.** At this stage, you've made a square base.

**8.**

Fold open and press down flap.

**7.**

Fold and unfold top flap.

*squash

**9.**

**10.**

Repeat steps 7–9 on remaining three flaps.

**11.**

Fold and unfold top flap.

**12.**

Open top layer and fold upward at the same time.

**13.**

**14.**

Repeat steps 11–13 on remaining three flaps.

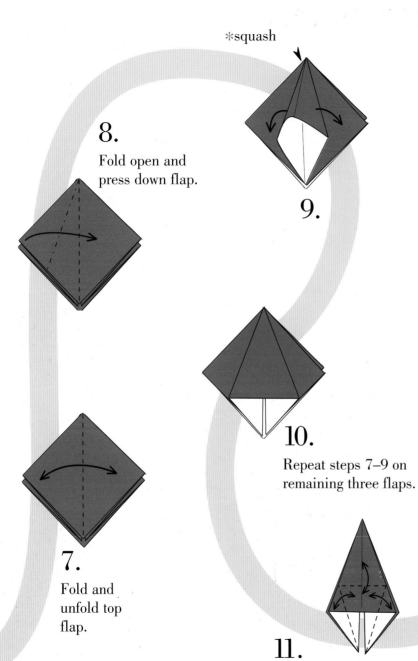
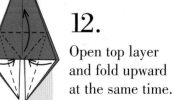

### 15.

*repeat

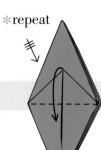

Fold corner of top layer down. Repeat on remaining three sides.

*rotate

## spring iris

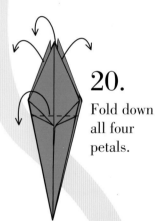

### 16.

Fold top flap, left to right.

### 20.

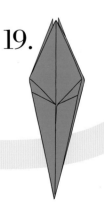

Fold down all four petals.

### 17.

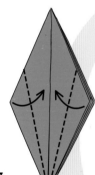

Fold left and right corners of top flap to the center.

### 18.

*repeat

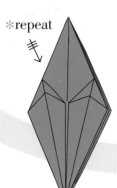

Repeat steps 16–18 on remaining three sides.

### 19.

# modular marigold

*Recommended paper*

*Cut two sheets of paper into quarters. Eight squares make a marigold.*

You may have made a chain from chewing gum wrappers at summer camp, but did you know that the principle of folding and interlocking paper can be applied to many other models? A favorite of mine is the Modular Marigold, created by the master of modularity, Mette Pedersen. Making it is like a combination of origami and knitting; the repetition as you fold is very soothing.

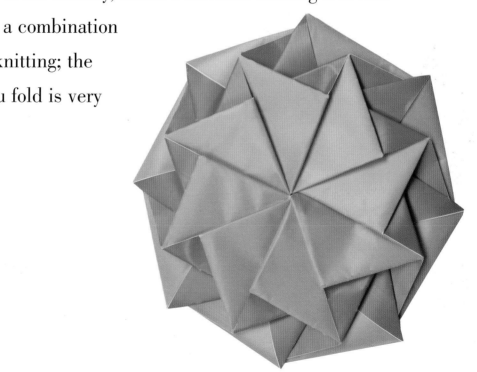

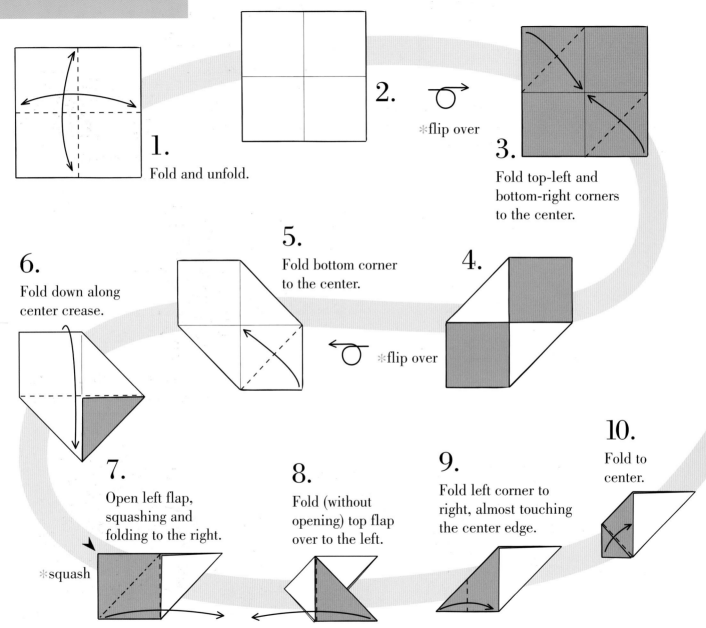

**1.** Fold and unfold.

**2.** ✳flip over

**3.** Fold top-left and bottom-right corners to the center.

**4.** ✳flip over

**5.** Fold bottom corner to the center.

**6.** Fold down along center crease.

**7.** Open left flap, squashing and folding to the right.

✳squash

**8.** Fold (without opening) top flap over to the left.

**9.** Fold left corner to right, almost touching the center edge.

**10.** Fold to center.

## 11.

Fold top left layer over to the right.

## 12.

A finished unit. Repeat steps 1–11 with 7 more sheets of paper.

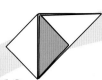

## 13.

Slide one unit into another: hook the hidden tab that's underneath the right flap of first unit into the pocket of the second unit.

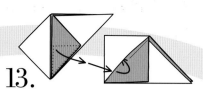

## 14.

Two connected units.

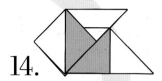

## 15.

Repeat steps 13 and 14 for each of the remaining flaps.

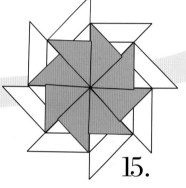

∗flip over

## 16.

Fold bottom right flap over to the left.

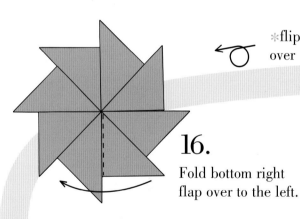

## 17.

Open and fold down the top layer of the right flap.

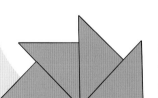

## 18.

Fold the flap back.

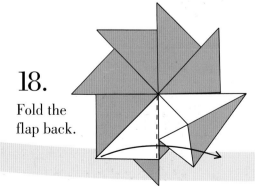

**24.**

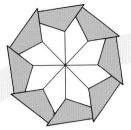

*flip over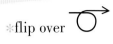

# modular marigold

by Mette Pedersen

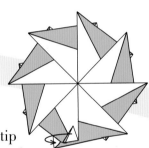

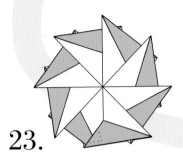

**23.**

Repeat steps 21 and 22 for the remaining flaps.

**22.**

Tuck folded tip into flap beneath.

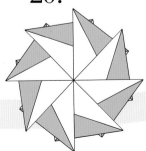

**19.**

Repeat steps 16–18 for the remaining flaps.

**20.**

**21.**

Fold tip so that it lies along the edge of the flap beneath.

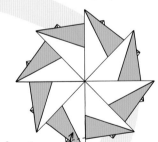

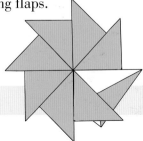

# simple swan

When it comes to fashionable origami, *simple* often says it best—especially for that most elegant of birds, the swan. And did you know that swans are among the most loyal birds in the animal kingdom? They mate for life. That makes the Simple Swan especially appropriate for wedding decorations or for an anniversary remembrance.

*Recommended paper*

# HOW TO FOLD THE SIMPLE SWAN

◆◇◇◇ LEVEL OF DIFFICULTY

**1.**
First, fold the paper in half and unfold. Second, fold left and right to center crease.

**2.**

**3.**
Fold left and right corners to center.

*flip over

**4.**
Fold bottom tip up to top tip.

**5.**
Fold tip down.

**6.**
Fold in half to back.

**7.**
Lift up head and neck.

*rotate

simple swan

# thirsty bird at the river of tranquillity

_Recommended paper_

Strangely enough, there's something wonderfully peaceful about an origami action model. This bright, yellow bird at the River of Tranquillity can have a calming influence on your day. Phone won't stop ringing? The world won't stop demanding? Take a timeout for this origami model. You'll feel much better— and so will a frantic loved one if you share it. Slip it into his or her briefcase as a reminder to slow down and enjoy the journey.

# How to fold the Thirsty Bird

◆◆◆◇ LEVEL OF DIFFICULTY

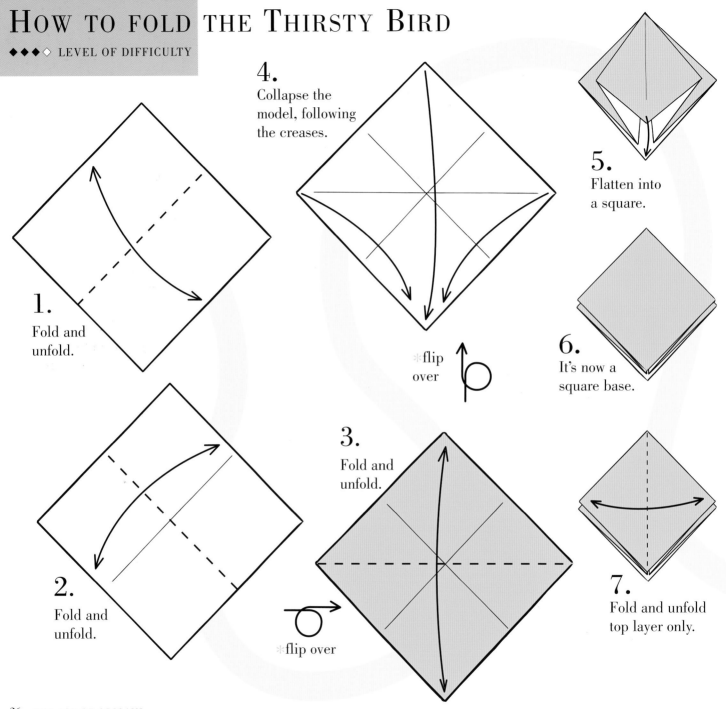

**1.** Fold and unfold.

**2.** Fold and unfold.

**3.** Fold and unfold.

*flip over

**4.** Collapse the model, following the creases.

*flip over

**5.** Flatten into a square.

**6.** It's now a square base.

**7.** Fold and unfold top layer only.

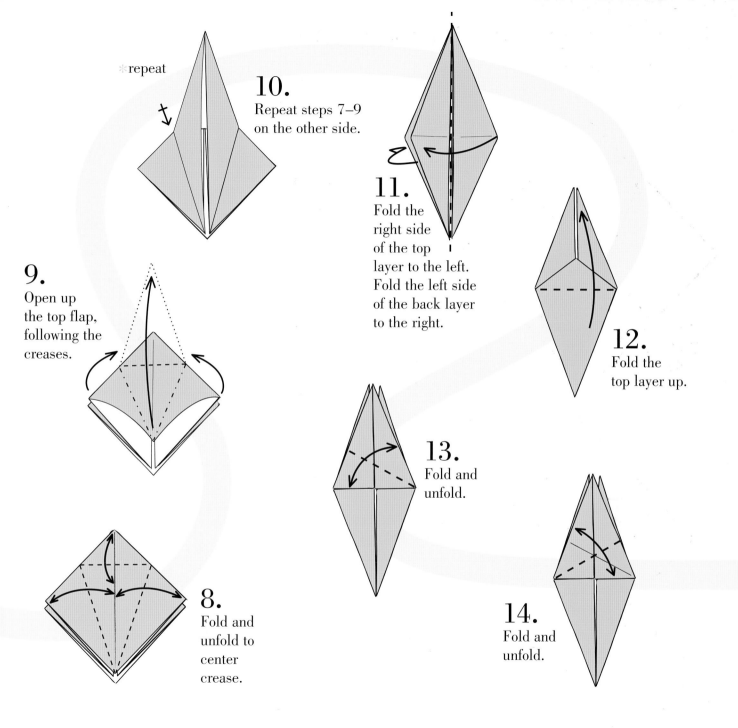

**repeat**

**10.**
Repeat steps 7–9
on the other side.

**9.**
Open up
the top flap,
following the
creases.

**8.**
Fold and
unfold to
center
crease.

**11.**
Fold the
right side
of the top
layer to the left.
Fold the left side
of the back layer
to the right.

**12.**
Fold the
top layer up.

**13.**
Fold and
unfold.

**14.**
Fold and
unfold.

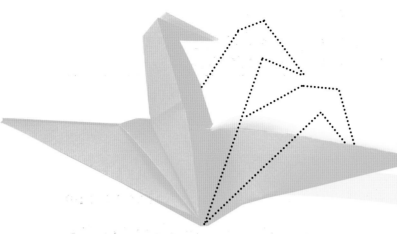

# thirsty bird
# at the river
# of tranquillity

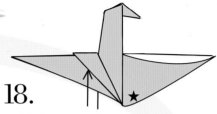

**18.**

Hold the water bowl with one hand. Insert your thumb and index finger of your other hand into the pockets. Now lift up and forward.

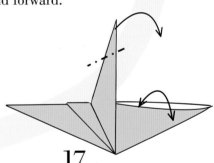

**17.**

Inside reverse fold to create head. Then open to shape water bowl.

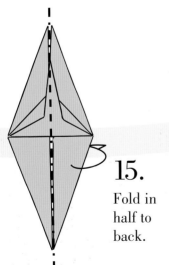

**15.**

Fold in half to back.

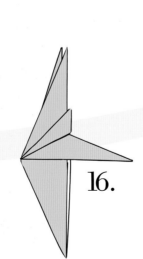

**16.**

*rotate

# pecking chicken

*Recommended paper*
*Cut the paper with*
*the small chickens into*
*quarters to fold four.*

This barnyard fowl is equally at home on the farm or in the cubicle of a busy office worker. It's true. The Pecking Chicken has been known to liven up an otherwise dull business meeting (especially when it's folded with our paper, designed by the fabulously nutty Robert Zimmerman). The model itself was created by the paper sculptor Paul Jackson, whose art has been exhibited in museums and shows around the world.

# HOW TO FOLD THE PECKING CHICKEN

◆◇◇◇ LEVEL OF DIFFICULTY

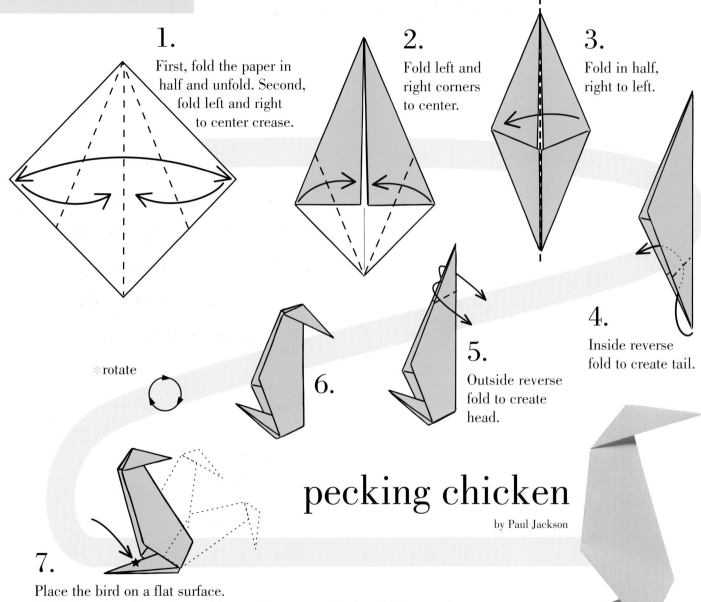

**1.**
First, fold the paper in half and unfold. Second, fold left and right to center crease.

**2.**
Fold left and right corners to center.

**3.**
Fold in half, right to left.

**4.**
Inside reverse fold to create tail.

**5.**
Outside reverse fold to create head.

*rotate

**6.**

**7.**
Place the bird on a flat surface.
Hold the tail and tap down with your finger to make the chicken peck.

pecking chicken
by Paul Jackson

# flapping bird of happiness

*Recommended paper*

If there's one sure-fire crowd-pleaser in the world of origami—this is it. It's guaranteed to put a smile on anyone's face. Want to thank someone for a special act of kindness or generosity? Want to share your feelings about some really good news? Now you can share the Flapping Bird of Happiness. Just be sure to share it in person so you can see the recipient's reaction. Fold it, flap it, flaunt it.

# HOW TO FOLD THE FLAPPING BIRD OF HAPPINESS

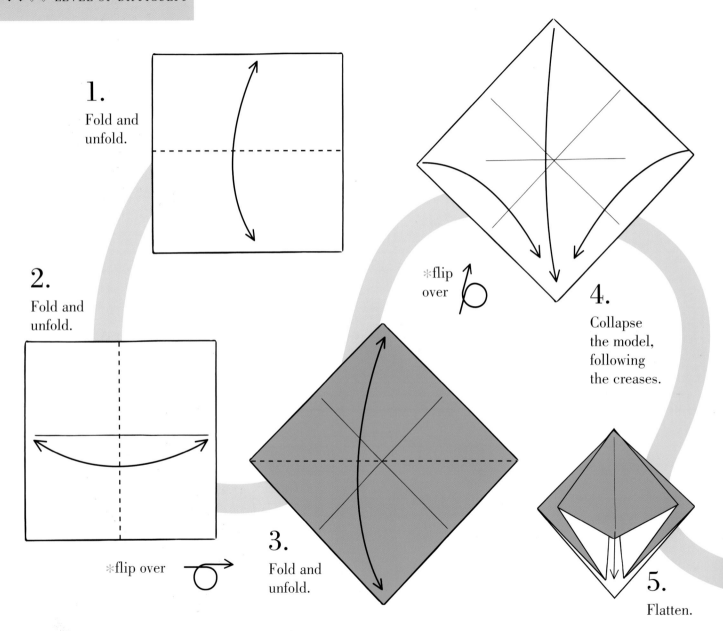

**1.**
Fold and unfold.

**2.**
Fold and unfold.

*flip over

**3.**
Fold and unfold.

**4.**
Collapse the model, following the creases.

*flip over

**5.**
Flatten.

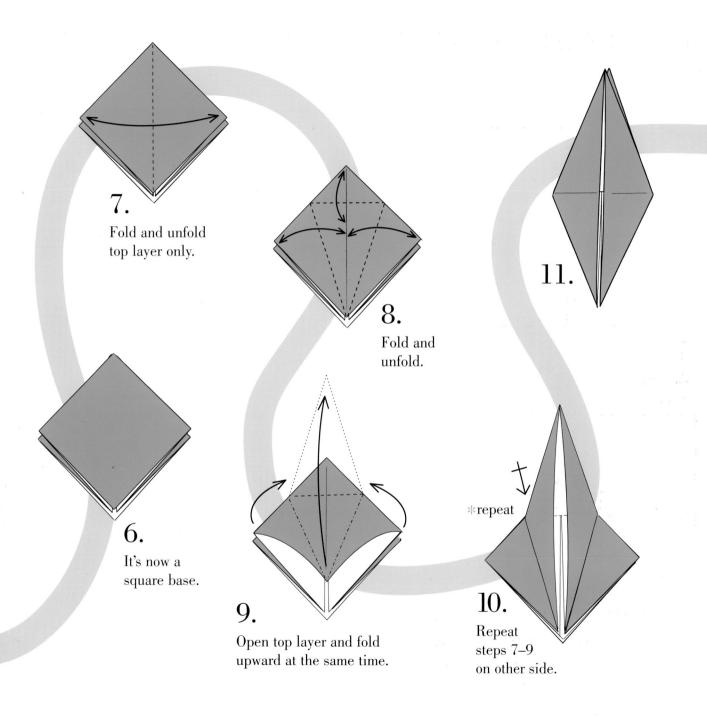

**7.**

Fold and unfold
top layer only.

**8.**

Fold and
unfold.

**11.**

**6.**

It's now a
square base.

**9.**

Open top layer and fold
upward at the same time.

*repeat

**10.**

Repeat
steps 7–9
on other side.

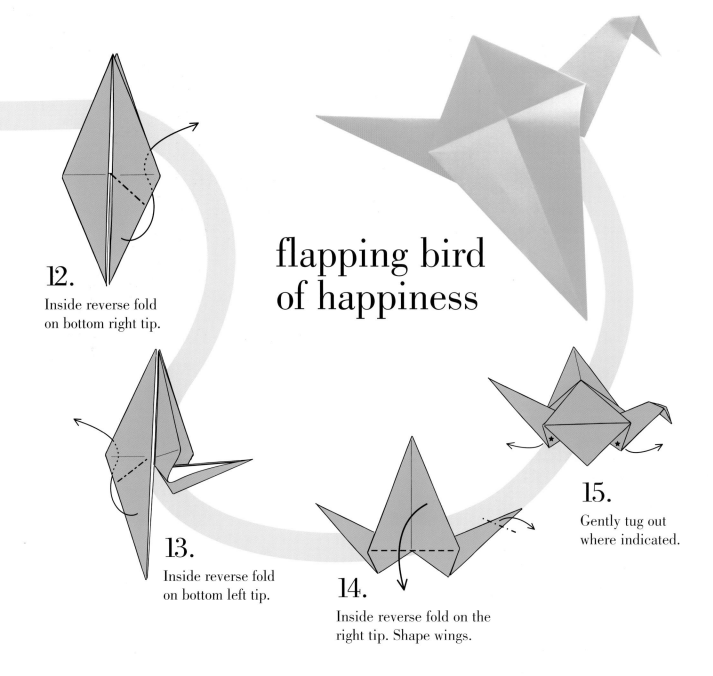

**12.**

Inside reverse fold on bottom right tip.

# flapping bird of happiness

**13.**

Inside reverse fold on bottom left tip.

**14.**

Inside reverse fold on the right tip. Shape wings.

**15.**

Gently tug out where indicated.

# urban bird

Here's something for all you city dwellers.
This bird can be seen wherever there
are people with crumbs: from St. Mark's
in Venice to good old 42nd Street.
Known as the rock dove to birders and the
pigeon to everyone else, this Urban Bird does altitude
with attitude. Our paper has a suitably cosmopolitan design
for this bird about town.

*Recommended paper*

# How to Fold the Urban Bird

◆◇◇ LEVEL OF DIFFICULTY

**6.**

Fold left corner down and unfold.

**1.**

Fold in half, left to right.

*repeat

**5.**

Inside reverse fold top flap. Repeat on other side.

**2.**

Fold in half, top to bottom.

*repeat

**4.**

Fold tip up to meet edge, then unfold. Repeat on other side.

*repeat

**3.**

Fold left tip up to meet right tip. Repeat on other side.

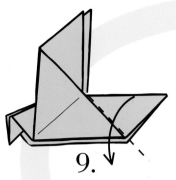

**9.**

Fold right corner down.

**10.**

Open top layer of tail, and squash fold.

*squash

**8.**

Open top layer up. Repeat on other side.

*repeat

**11.**

Fold right half back.

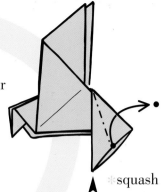

**7.**

Inside reverse fold to make the head.

# urban bird

# dollar
# bunny

Leave this cutie for your favorite waiter or waitress!

◆◆◇◇ LEVEL OF DIFFICULTY

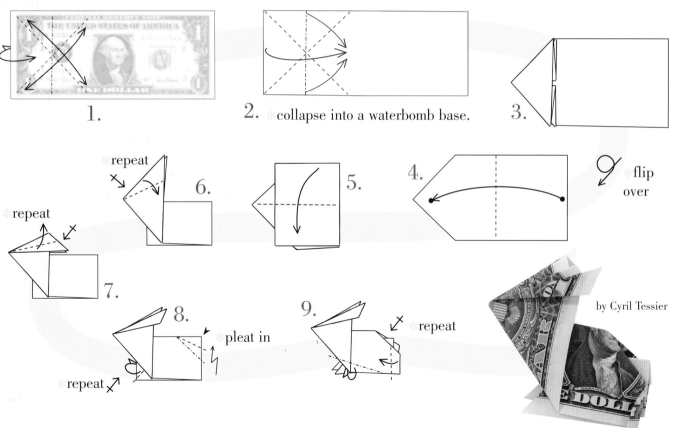

1.

2. * collapse into a waterbomb base.

3.

* flip over

4.

5.

* repeat

6.

* repeat

7.

8. * pleat in

* repeat

9. * repeat

by Cyril Tessier

# cliff swallow

In the world of origami, Robert J. Lang is one of the Great Ones. A pioneer of the cross-disciplinary marriage of origami with mathematics, Dr. Lang had a successful career as a physicist and engineer before becoming a full-time origami artist.

He has created more than 450 origami designs, including some of the most complex models ever made. The Cliff Swallow is one of Dr. Lang's less complex models, with his hallmark of beautifully detailed realism.

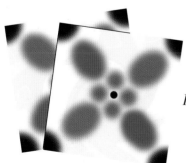

*Recommended paper*

# How to fold the Cliff Swallow

◆◆◆◆ LEVEL OF DIFFICULTY

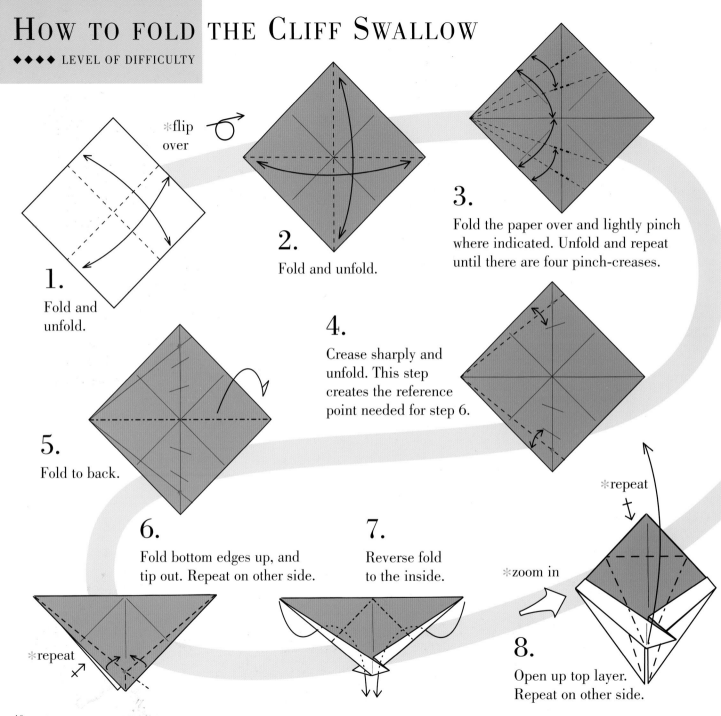

*flip over

**1.**

Fold and unfold.

**2.**

Fold and unfold.

**3.**

Fold the paper over and lightly pinch where indicated. Unfold and repeat until there are four pinch-creases.

**4.**

Crease sharply and unfold. This step creates the reference point needed for step 6.

**5.**

Fold to back.

**6.**

Fold bottom edges up, and tip out. Repeat on other side.

*repeat

**7.**

Reverse fold to the inside.

**8.**

Open up top layer. Repeat on other side.

*repeat

*zoom in

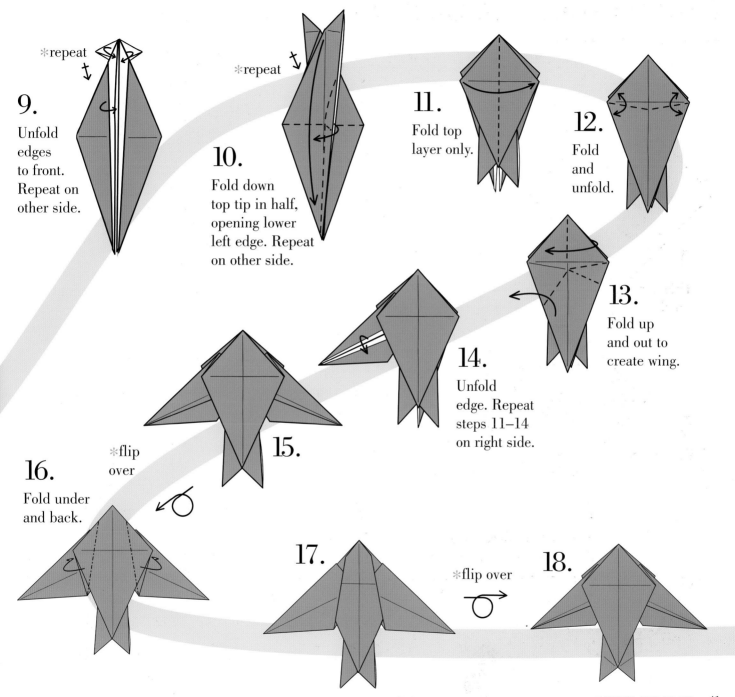

**9.**
Unfold edges to front. Repeat on other side.

*repeat

**10.**
Fold down top tip in half, opening lower left edge. Repeat on other side.

*repeat

**11.**
Fold top layer only.

**12.**
Fold and unfold.

**13.**
Fold up and out to create wing.

**14.**
Unfold edge. Repeat steps 11–14 on right side.

**15.**

*flip over

**16.**
Fold under and back.

**17.**

*flip over

**18.**

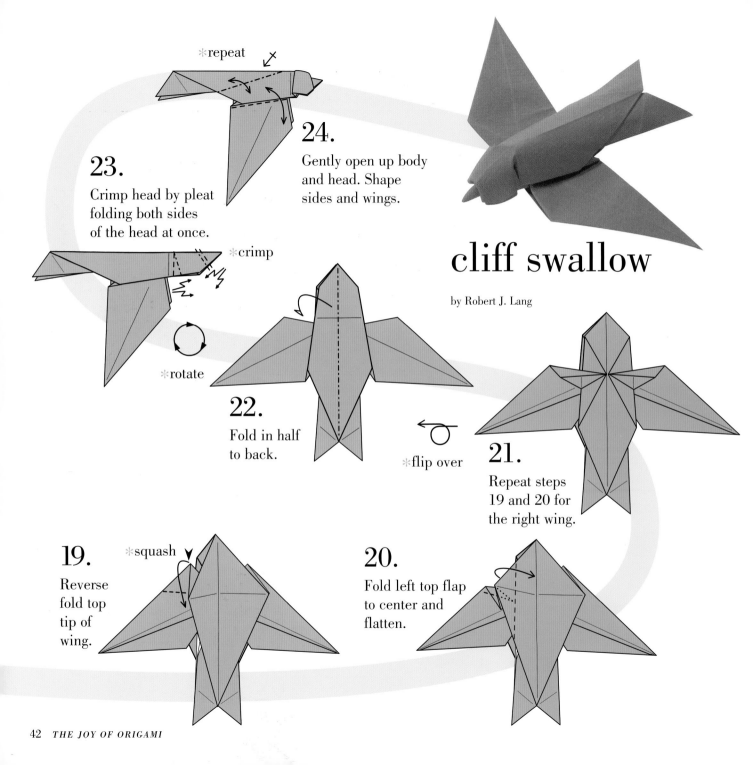

**23.**

Crimp head by pleat folding both sides of the head at once.

✳repeat

**24.**

Gently open up body and head. Shape sides and wings.

✳crimp

✳rotate

# cliff swallow

by Robert J. Lang

**22.**

Fold in half to back.

✳flip over

**21.**

Repeat steps 19 and 20 for the right wing.

**19.**

Reverse fold top tip of wing.

✳squash

**20.**

Fold left top flap to center and flatten.

# kissing cranes

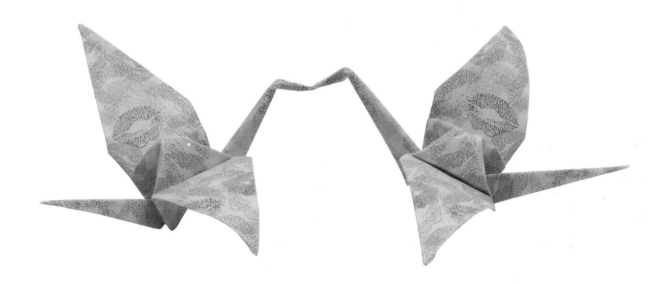

*Recommended paper*

Share a little love with the Kissing Cranes, an ancient origami from Japan. This model is made from a single sheet of paper, just as one love is made from two hearts. Of course, love is also made from many kisses and our paper has kisses galore! So make this pair of cranes today and maybe something sweet will swoop down on you.

# How to fold the Kissing Cranes

◆◆◆◆ LEVEL OF DIFFICULTY

To start, cut your square paper in half.

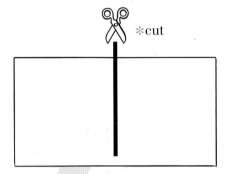

## 1.

Cut in half again, almost to the tip, so that there are two barely attached squares.

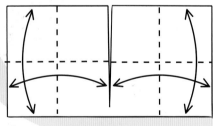

## 2.

On both squares, fold in half, bottom to top and left and right. Unfold.

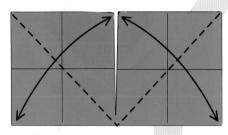

## 3.

Fold both squares in half, diagonally. Unfold.

*flip over

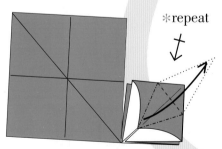

## 4.

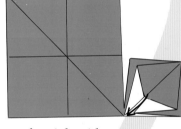

## 5.

Collapse the right side following creases.

*repeat

## 6.

Fold top layer up, creasing the sides in. Repeat on the back side.

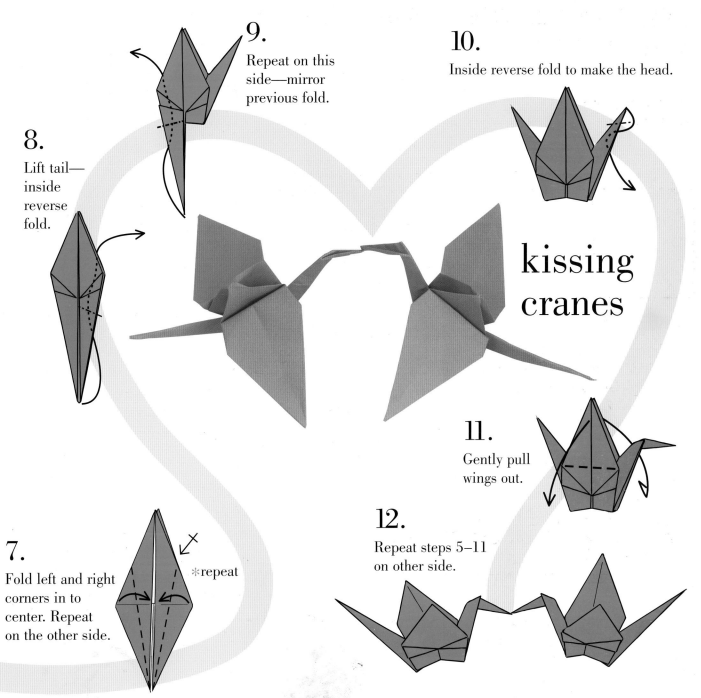

**9.**
Repeat on this side—mirror previous fold.

**10.**
Inside reverse fold to make the head.

**8.**
Lift tail—inside reverse fold.

# kissing cranes

**7.**
Fold left and right corners in to center. Repeat on the other side.

*repeat

**11.**
Gently pull wings out.

**12.**
Repeat steps 5–11 on other side.

# printer paper gnasher

Take a piece of paper out of your computer printer tray and make a gnasher puppet. Caution: he bites!

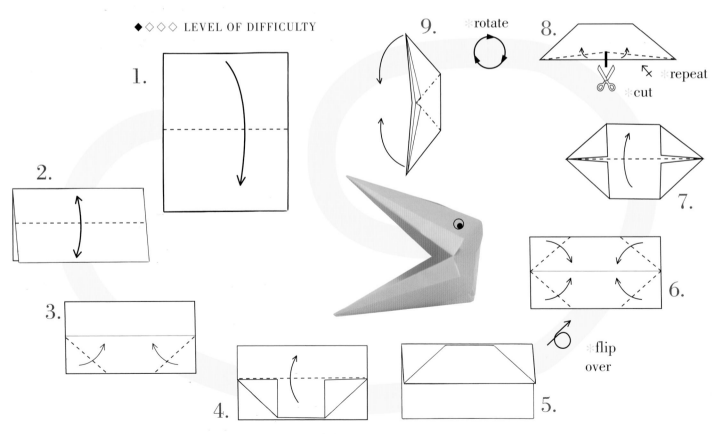

◆◇◇◇ LEVEL OF DIFFICULTY

1.

2.

3.

4.

5.

6.

*flip over

7.

8. *cut *repeat

9. *rotate

# toucan beak

*Recommended paper*

Need a silly party favor? Or a quick disguise at the zoo? This model was designed by one of the all-time origami masters, Kunihiko Kasahara (just check out his magnificent Tyrannosaurus Rex on page 129). As you can see, our paper is zoologically accurate and it's also foolproof for folding. To wear the Toucan Beak, cut a rubber band, poke two holes in the model, and knot both ends of the rubber band through the holes. Voilà! Now you can really follow your nose.

# How to fold the Toucan Beak

◆◆◇◇ LEVEL OF DIFFICULTY

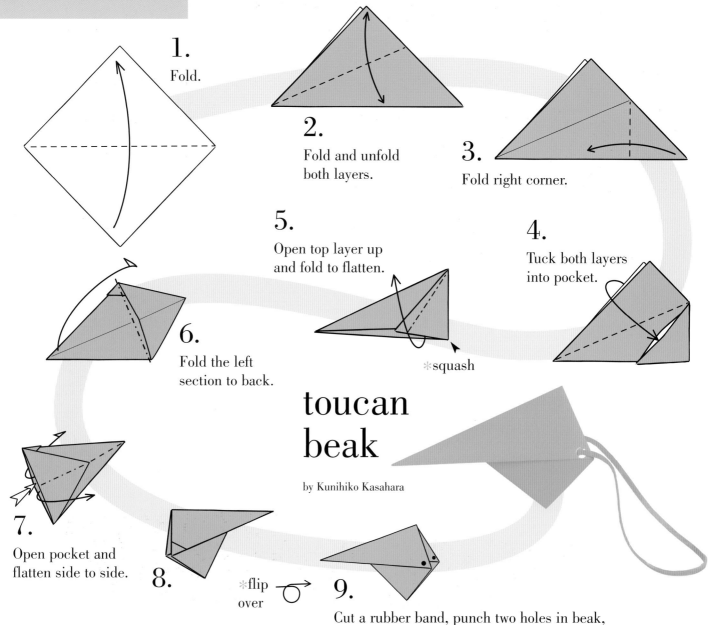

**1.**
Fold.

**2.**
Fold and unfold both layers.

**3.**
Fold right corner.

**5.**
Open top layer up and fold to flatten.

**4.**
Tuck both layers into pocket.

*squash

**6.**
Fold the left section to back.

# toucan beak

by Kunihiko Kasahara

**7.**
Open pocket and flatten side to side.

**8.**

*flip over

**9.**
Cut a rubber band, punch two holes in beak, and string the rubber band through the holes.

# twin sailboats

*Recommended paper*

Ahoy there! A briny breeze, gentle waves, and the tastiest lemonade ever! Nothing is better than a sunny afternoon of sailing. But for those times when a billowing canvas just isn't on the horizon, here's a model to remember it by. With four folds, these sweet little boats will transport you to that magical afternoon.

# How to fold the Twin Sailboats

◆◇◇◇ LEVEL OF DIFFICULTY

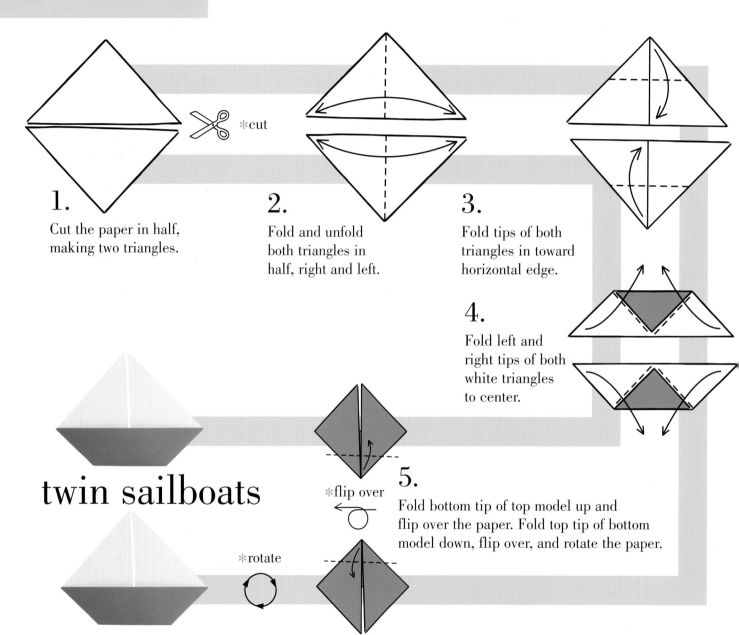

**1.**
Cut the paper in half, making two triangles.

**2.**
Fold and unfold both triangles in half, right and left.

**3.**
Fold tips of both triangles in toward horizontal edge.

**4.**
Fold left and right tips of both white triangles to center.

**5.**
Fold bottom tip of top model up and flip over the paper. Fold top tip of bottom model down, flip over, and rotate the paper.

*cut

*flip over

*rotate

twin sailboats

# sinking ship

Origami came from Japan, but, like American blue jeans, it now belongs to the world. One of the great designers from the Spanish-speaking world (Colombia, to be specific) is José Tomas Buitrago, a professor of engineering. His Sinking Ship is one of the funniest models I know. Is it a representation of a day at the office or a reminder that amateurs made the Ark and professionals made the Titanic? No doubt you'll find your own meaning in this model, which is bound to raise some smiles.

*Recommended paper*

# HOW TO FOLD THE SINKING SHIP

◆◆◇◇ LEVEL OF DIFFICULTY

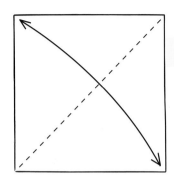

## 1.

Fold top left corner down
to meet bottom right corner.
Unfold.

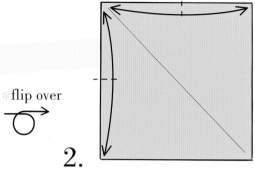

*flip over

## 2.

Fold and unfold top and left side.
Crease to match dotted lines
in step 3.

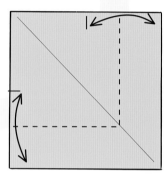

## 3.

Fold right side and bottom to the
creases just made. Crease from
the edges to the diagonal.

*flip over

## 4.

Fold along creases: the diagonal
folds in, and the lines to the left
and below it fold out.

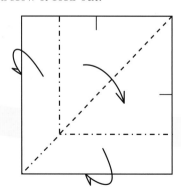

## 5.

Fold tip down to
bottom corner.

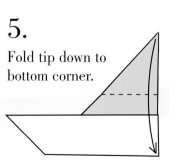

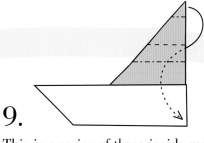

## 9.

This is a series of three inside reverse folds. Fold tip to meet bottom right corner. Pull and fold up cabin. Fold tip down to complete the smokestack.

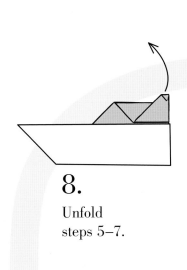

## 8.

Unfold steps 5–7.

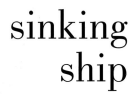

## 10.

Fold the top layer in. Repeat on other side.

## 7.

Fold tip down.

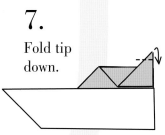

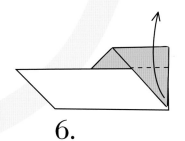

*repeat

## 11.

Fold the top layer of the protruding triangle in. Repeat on other side.

*rotate

## 6.

Fold tip up.

# sinking ship

by José Tomas Buitrago

# royal crown

Start with four sheets of printer paper or use the sheets in the origami paper section.

This model is by the queen of origami crowns, Laura Kruskal.

◆◇◇◇ LEVEL OF DIFFICULTY

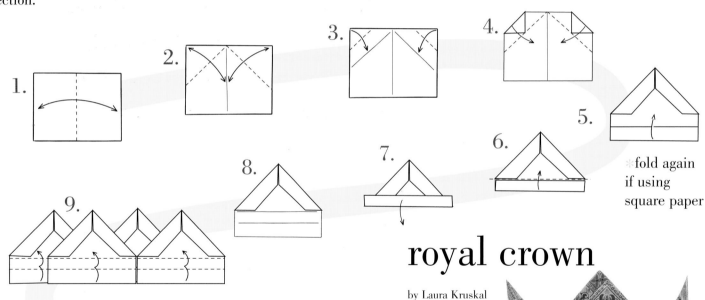

5. ✳ fold again if using square paper

## royal crown

by Laura Kruskal

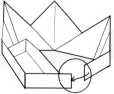

You can also use the paper we've included.

# ship of 1,000 cranes

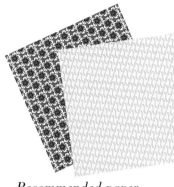

*Recommended paper*

This ship is one of the wonders of the origami world. Until the very last move, a dramatic pullout, no one can tell what you're folding. Then (drum roll, please!) from a much-folded rectangle, a ship suddenly appears! Fold it in company and you're sure to get a standing ovation. Our paper has 1,000 cranes—a symbol of peace in origami lore. What? Don't see the 1,000 cranes? Look closer!

# How to fold the Ship of 1,000 Cranes

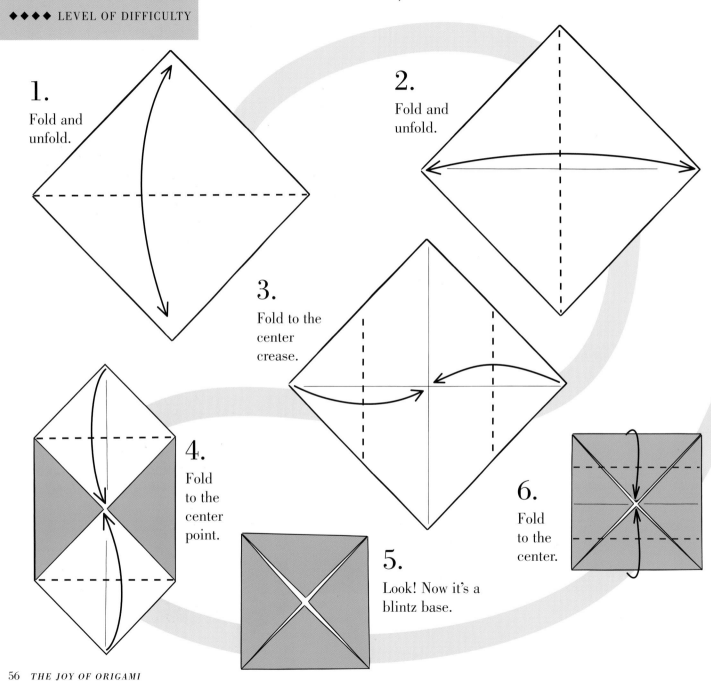

**1.** Fold and unfold.

**2.** Fold and unfold.

**3.** Fold to the center crease.

**4.** Fold to the center point.

**5.** Look! Now it's a blintz base.

**6.** Fold to the center.

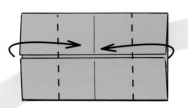

## 7.

Fold to the center.

## 8.

Fold and unfold
the diagonals.

## 9.

Reach in
and pull
out inner
flap.

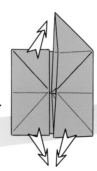

## 10.

Pull out
remaining
three flaps.

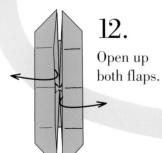

## 11.

Fold to back.

## 12.

Open up
both flaps.

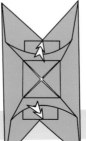

## 13.

Pull out and
flatten the
raised center
points.

## 14.

Gently unfold and open
up the left and right sides.
(Be careful not to pull
apart the folds
on the back
side.)

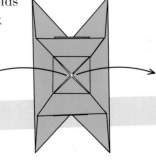

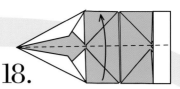

## 18.

Fold in half,
bottom to top.

## 19.

Magic time! Hold with
both hands. Slowly pull
both sides out and up.
Crazy, isn't it?

## 17.

On the left side, fold
in the corner points.
Fold the right edge left.

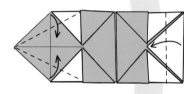

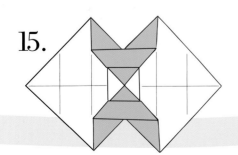

# ship of 1,000 cranes

## 16.

Fold top flaps down, bottom flaps
up, and right-most flap to the left.

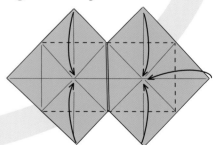

## 15.

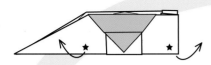

*flip
over

# patient dog

Let's fold one for everyone's best friend. Few sights in life are as touching as seeing your dog patiently waiting for a walk, a scratch behind the ear, or a little taste of that leftover meatloaf. Origami master Anita Barbour perfectly captures the essence of a dog's faithful vigil in her model, Patient Dog. And it's surprisingly simple. The trickiest part is the nose, but don't worry. We'll take it a fold at a time. Patient Dog is the perfect origami surprise for a fellow dog lover—or for someone who's been keeping you waiting!

*Recommended paper*

# How to Fold the Patient Dog

◆◆◇◇ LEVEL OF DIFFICULTY

## 1.

First, fold the paper in half and unfold. Second, fold left and right to center crease.

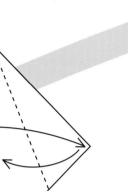

## 2.

Fold tip up.

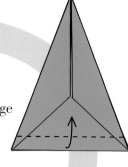

## 3.

Fold the bottom edge up about ½".

## 4.

Fold in half, right to left.

## 5.

Fold the corner up on the top layer only.

## 6.

Fold the top layer to the left. Repeat steps 5 and 6 on the other side.

∗repeat

∗rotate

## 7.

Precrease as shown and then crimp neck by pleat folding both sides at once.

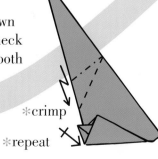

∗crimp

∗repeat

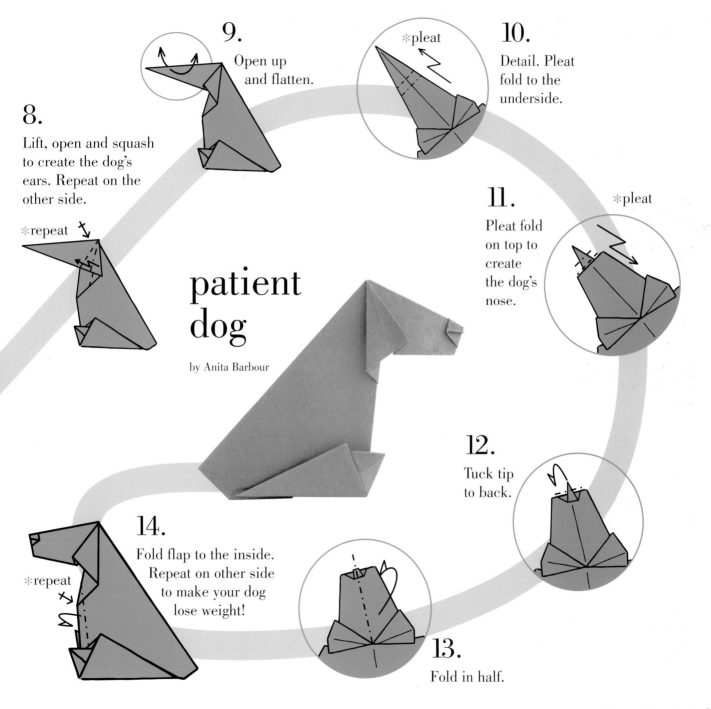

**8.**

Lift, open and squash to create the dog's ears. Repeat on the other side.

*repeat

**9.**

Open up and flatten.

**10.**

Detail. Pleat fold to the underside.

*pleat

**11.**

Pleat fold on top to create the dog's nose.

*pleat

# patient dog

by Anita Barbour

**12.**

Tuck tip to back.

**13.**

Fold in half.

**14.**

Fold flap to the inside. Repeat on other side to make your dog lose weight!

*repeat

# dollar snail

Start with a crisp, new dollar bill and take it slow!

◆◆◆◇ LEVEL OF DIFFICULTY

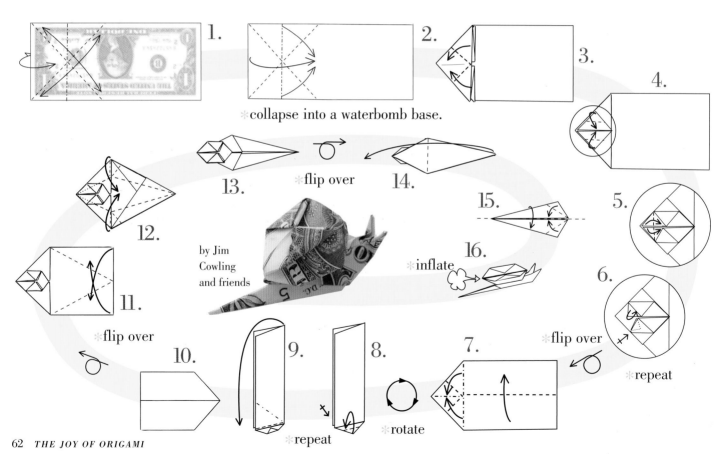

1.

2.

*collapse into a waterbomb base.

3.

4.

13.

*flip over

14.

15.

5.

12.

by Jim
Cowling
and friends

16.

*inflate

6.

11.

*flip over

10.

9.

8.

7.

*flip over

*repeat

*repeat

*rotate

# furry cat

Many origami people are also cat people. Maybe it's because folders love a mystery, and nothing on earth is as mysterious as the cat. Why, for instance, does she wait until you're almost finished with a complicated fold to jump up and flatten your origami model? On the other hand, there's nothing too mysterious about the Furry Cat. She just seems pleased to be in your company (to be on the safe side, though, you might check to see if the canary is still in its cage).

*Recommended paper*

# How to fold the Furry Cat

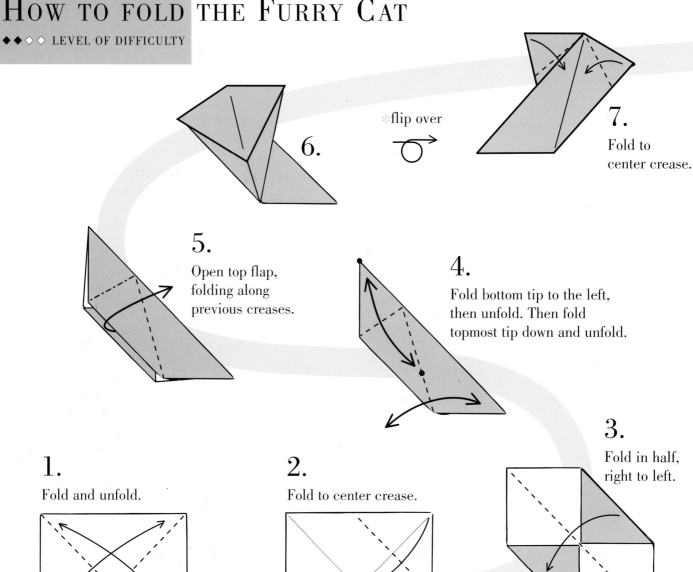

**6.**

*flip over

**7.**
Fold to
center crease.

**5.**
Open top flap,
folding along
previous creases.

**4.**
Fold bottom tip to the left,
then unfold. Then fold
topmost tip down and unfold.

**3.**
Fold in half,
right to left.

**1.**
Fold and unfold.

**2.**
Fold to center crease.

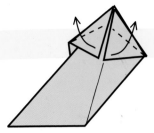

**8.**

Fold tips up to make the cat's ears.

**9.**

Fold and unfold bottom left tip. Fold topmost tip twice and tuck under the ears.

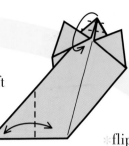

*flip over

# furry cat

*draw eyes to match your cat's personality

**10.**

Fold tip up to make the cat's snout.

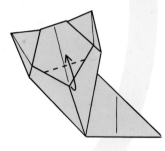

**13.**

Fold out on the underside, following the creases.

**11.**

Fold tip down.

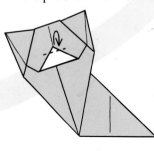

**12.**

Fold to back.

# business reply card fish

Karen Reeds is one of the world's leading folders using "found paper." Her fish, using a reply card, is one of my favorite models.

◆◆◇◇ LEVEL OF DIFFICULTY

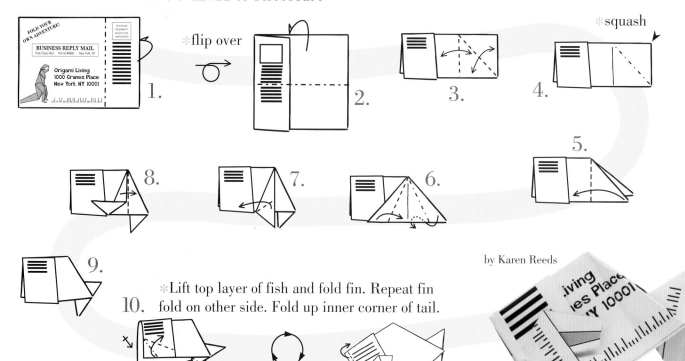

*flip over

*squash

*Lift top layer of fish and fold fin. Repeat fin fold on other side. Fold up inner corner of tail.

*repeat

*rotate

by Karen Reeds

# weiner dog

*Recommended paper*

I'm a dog person with a special fondness for those bright-eyed dachshunds. What could be cuter? This model by Susanna Kricskovics perfectly captures the beloved Weiner Dog, from its stubby legs to its elongated body. So long, in fact, that it takes two pieces of paper to make the model's body. Our paper employs a pattern to make the model a real hot dog!

# How to fold the Weiner Dog

◆◆◇◇ **LEVEL OF DIFFICULTY**

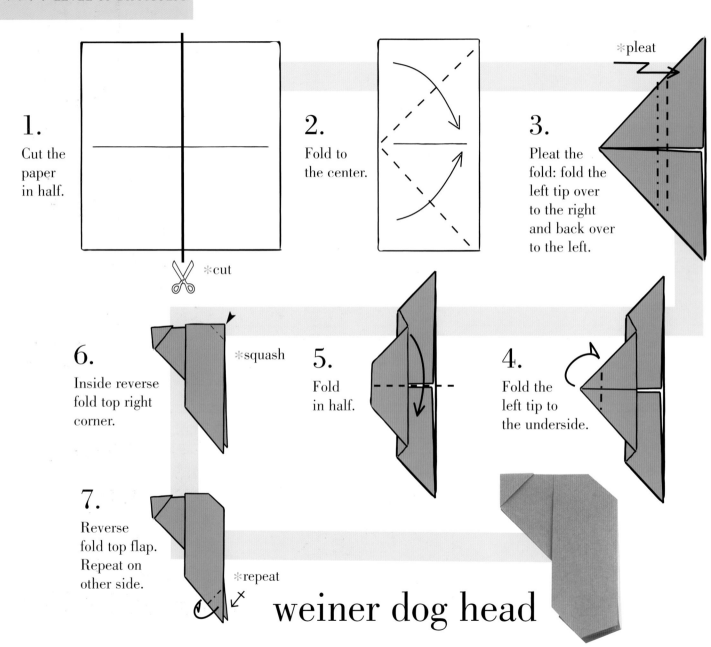

**1.**
Cut the paper in half.

∗cut

**2.**
Fold to the center.

**3.**
Pleat the fold: fold the left tip over to the right and back over to the left.

∗pleat

**4.**
Fold the left tip to the underside.

**5.**
Fold in half.

**6.**
Inside reverse fold top right corner.

∗squash

**7.**
Reverse fold top flap. Repeat on other side.

∗repeat

weiner dog head

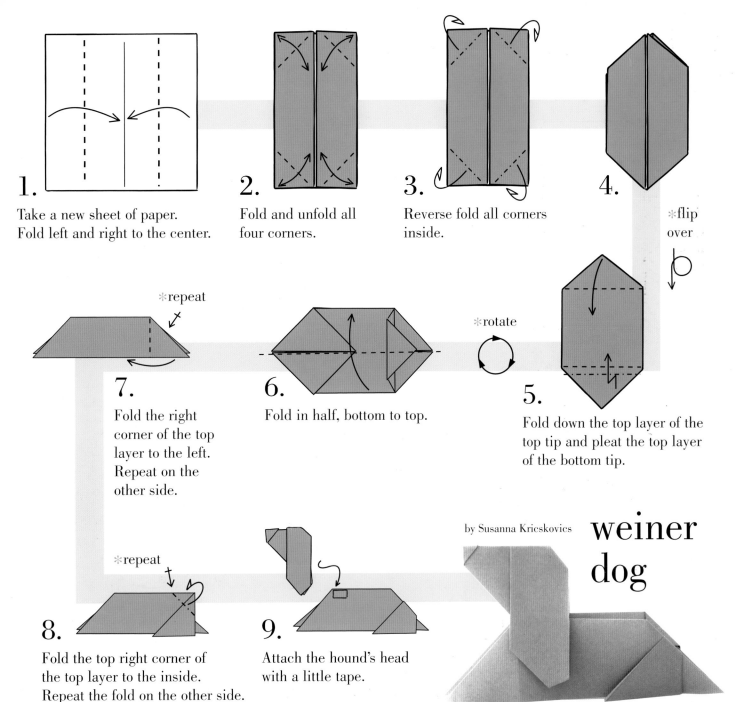

**1.**
Take a new sheet of paper.
Fold left and right to the center.

**2.**
Fold and unfold all
four corners.

**3.**
Reverse fold all corners
inside.

**4.**

*flip
over

**7.**
Fold the right
corner of the top
layer to the left.
Repeat on the
other side.

*repeat

**6.**
Fold in half, bottom to top.

*rotate

**5.**
Fold down the top layer of the
top tip and pleat the top layer
of the bottom tip.

**8.**
Fold the top right corner of
the top layer to the inside.
Repeat the fold on the other side.

*repeat

**9.**
Attach the hound's head
with a little tape.

by Susanna Kricskovics **weiner
dog**

# newspaper hat

This is the classic model that's always in style!

◆◇◇◇ LEVEL OF DIFFICULTY

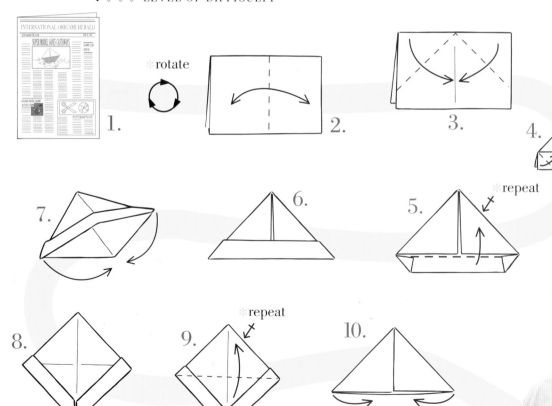

# loving heart

*Recommended paper*

Say it with words, by all means, but to really get your message across, say it with origami. When it comes to giving a sign of affection, turn to Francis Ow, the all-time master of the origami heart. His model, Loving Heart, is a wonderful Valentine for any time of year. So don't be shy. Say it with origami today.

# How to fold the Loving Heart

◆◆◇◇ LEVEL OF DIFFICULTY

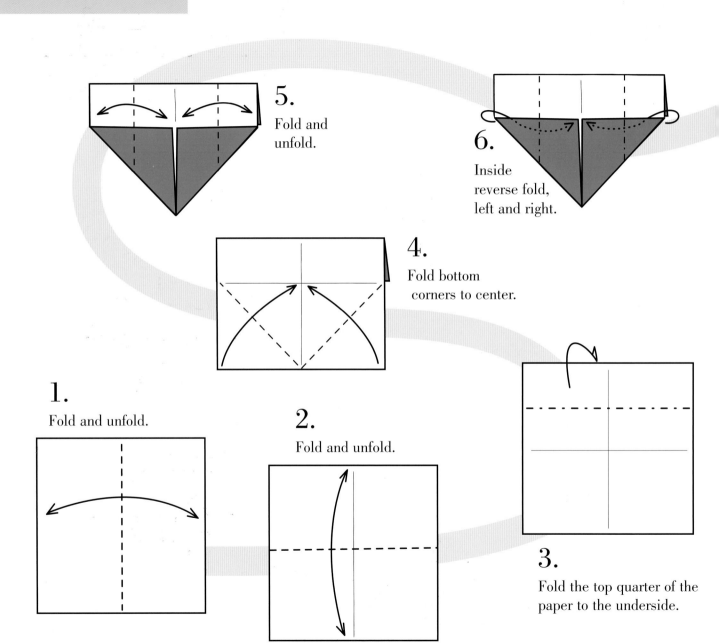

**5.** Fold and unfold.

**6.** Inside reverse fold, left and right.

**4.** Fold bottom corners to center.

**1.** Fold and unfold.

**2.** Fold and unfold.

**3.** Fold the top quarter of the paper to the underside.

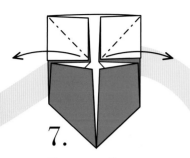

**7.**

Open top flaps
to the outside.

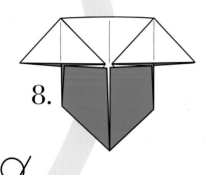

**8.**

*flip
over

**9.**

Fold
bottom
tip to
the top.

**10.**

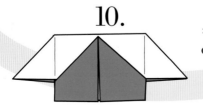

*flip
over

**13.**

Fold top tips down.
Fold and unfold
top layer only.

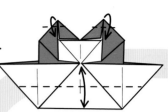

*rotate

**12.**

Fold tips up.
Rotate.

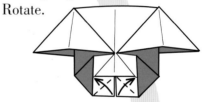

**11.**

Open flaps down.

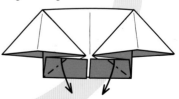

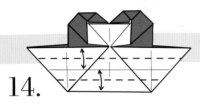

## 14.

Fold and unfold: bottom edge to center crease and center crease to top edge.

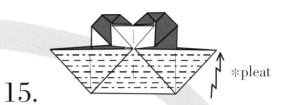

*pleat

## 15.

Pleat bottom section, folding under, then up. Your last fold should be an underfold.

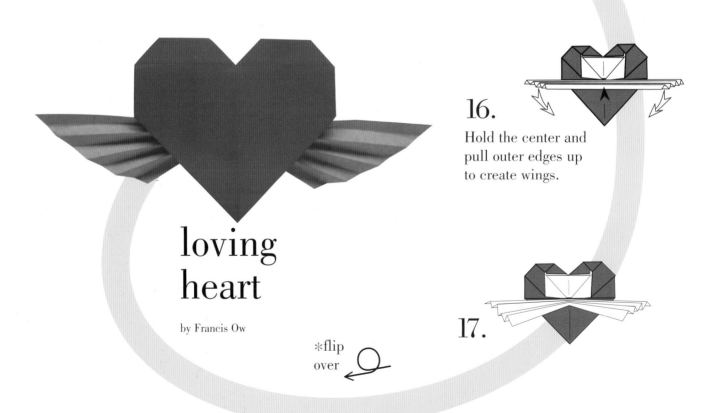

## 16.

Hold the center and pull outer edges up to create wings.

## 17.

# loving heart

by Francis Ow

*flip over

# stars and stripes pinwheel

*Recommended paper*

Three cheers for the red, white, and blue! Get those burgers on the grill, the soda on ice, the croquet hoops in place, and have yourself an all-American summer day. Just one more thing. To catch those summer breezes, fold yourself a patriotic pinwheel. The spinning stars and stripes will make any gathering more festive (and it's safer than fireworks). Even the youngest child is fascinated by a pinwheel. Enlist a child to help you fold one, and make an origami fan for life.

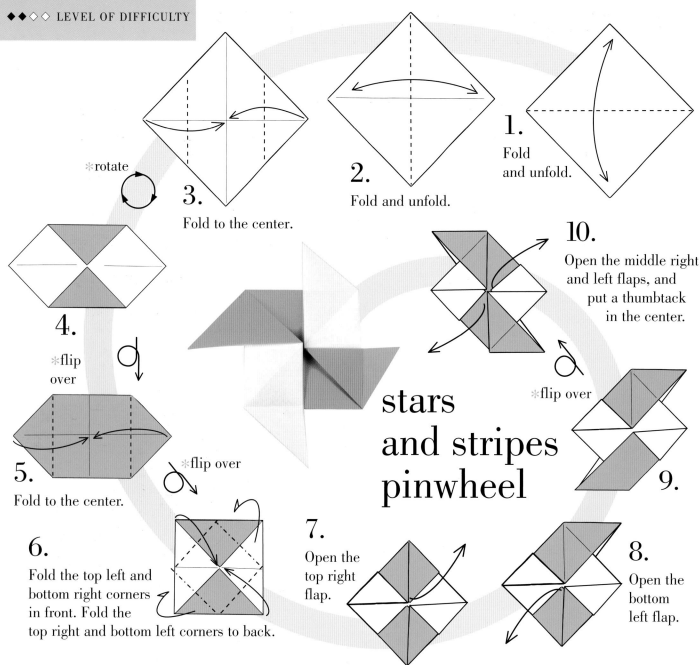

# HOW TO FOLD THE STARS AND STRIPES PINWHEEL

◆◆◇◇ LEVEL OF DIFFICULTY

**1.**
Fold
and unfold.

**2.**
Fold and unfold.

**3.**
Fold to the center.

✳rotate

**4.**

✳flip over

**5.**
Fold to the center.

✳flip over

**6.**
Fold the top left and
bottom right corners
in front. Fold the
top right and bottom left corners to back.

**7.**
Open the
top right
flap.

**8.**
Open the
bottom
left flap.

**9.**

✳flip over

**10.**
Open the middle right
and left flaps, and
put a thumbtack
in the center.

## stars
## and stripes
## pinwheel

# summer basket

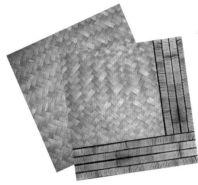

*Recommended paper*

A basket is a lovely decorative touch that says "country living"—even if you live in a basement apartment in a big city. The sight of a basket suggests apple-picking, flower-gathering, and tomatoes ripe for the plucking.

Our Summer Basket won't hold an apple, but it looks great—especially with our wicker-patterned paper.

Actually, I should say *they* look great, because this is a two-for-one deal!

# HOW TO FOLD THE SUMMER BASKET

◆◆◆◇ LEVEL OF DIFFICULTY

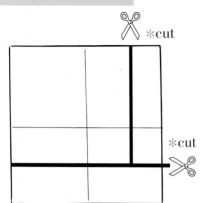

✄ *cut

*cut ✄

## 1.

Cut two strips as indicated by the black rules.

## 2.

Use the two strips to make the handles. Fold in half, and unfold.

## 3.

Fold top and bottom to the center crease.

## 4.

Fold in half.

## 5.

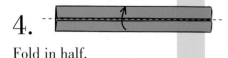

Save the handle to put on the basket.

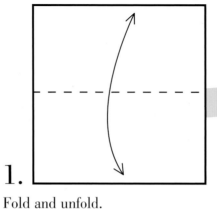

## 1.

Fold and unfold.

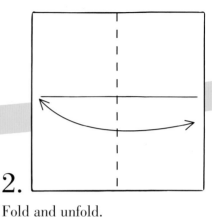

## 2.

Fold and unfold.

## 14.

Continue to pull out the flaps while flattening the bottom of the basket.

▲ *squash

## 13.

Pull out the flaps.

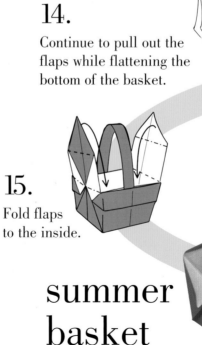

## 15.

Fold flaps to the inside.

# summer basket

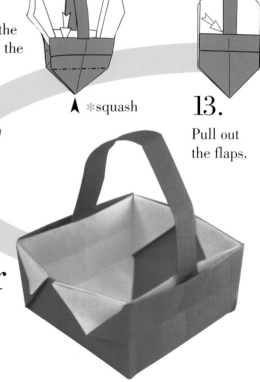

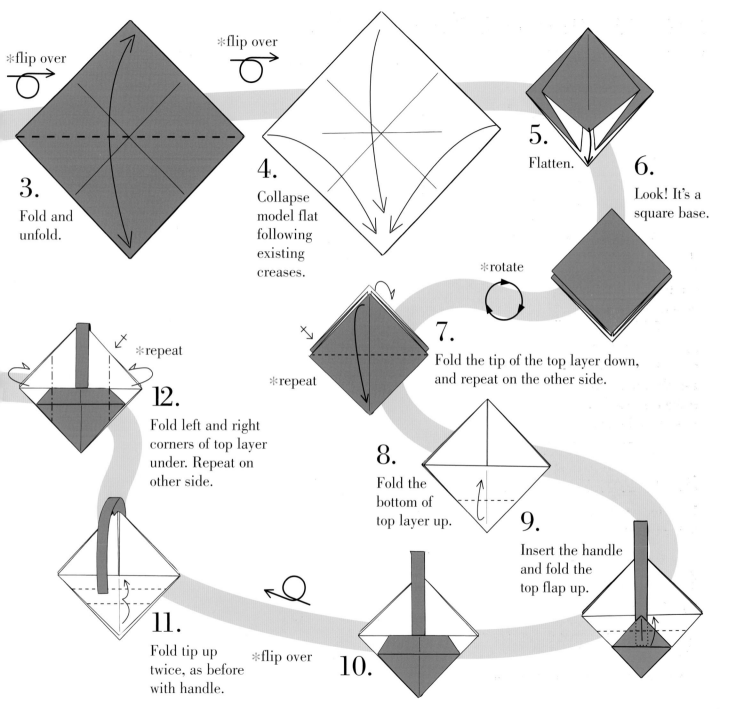

*flip over

*flip over

**3.**
Fold and
unfold.

**4.**
Collapse
model flat
following
existing
creases.

**5.**
Flatten.

**6.**
Look! It's a
square base.

*rotate

**7.**
Fold the tip of the top layer down,
and repeat on the other side.

*repeat

*repeat

**8.**
Fold the
bottom of
top layer up.

**9.**
Insert the handle
and fold the
top flap up.

**12.**
Fold left and right
corners of top layer
under. Repeat on
other side.

**11.**
Fold tip up
twice, as before
with handle.

*flip over

**10.**

# little
# saint nick

Have some gift wrap? Cut a square and make a Santa in just two folds!

◆◇◇◇ LEVEL OF DIFFICULTY

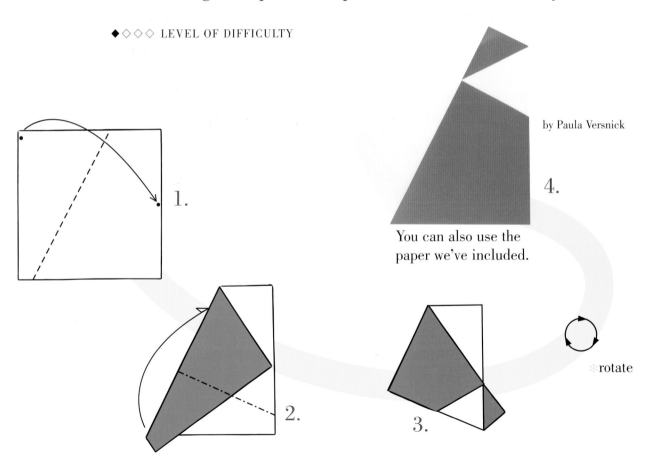

by Paula Versnick

1.

2.

3.

4.

You can also use the
paper we've included.

✳rotate

# trick-or-treat bat

*Recommended paper*

Bats should picket Hollywood! For decades, ever since Bela Lugosi first put on a cape, bats have been portrayed as creepy bloodsuckers instead of the helpful insectivores that they are. Florence Temko helps set things straight with an origami Trick-or-Treat Bat. He's a cute little guy. Of course, you should still feel free to use him as a Halloween decoration. This bat is a treat all the way.

# How to fold the Trick-or-Treat Bat

◆◆◇◇ LEVEL OF DIFFICULTY

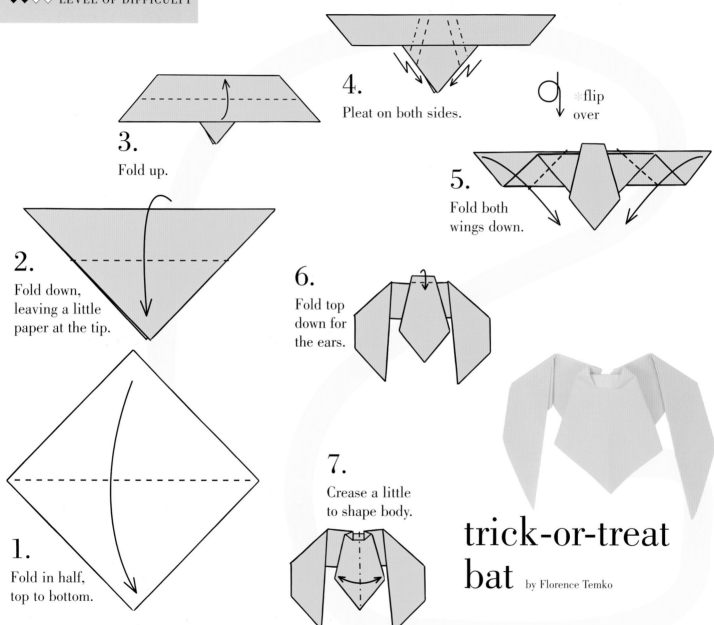

**4.**

Pleat on both sides.

⟳ ✳flip over

**3.**

Fold up.

**5.**

Fold both wings down.

**2.**

Fold down, leaving a little paper at the tip.

**6.**

Fold top down for the ears.

**7.**

Crease a little to shape body.

**1.**

Fold in half, top to bottom.

## trick-or-treat bat by Florence Temko

# leprechaun hat

*Recommended paper*

Top o' the morning to you! Here's a lucky find, a jaunty leprechaun hat. You don't have to be Irish for the leprechaun's magic to rub off on you. Fold it and share it with someone who could use a little magic from the end of a rainbow. Our paper has a green shamrock pattern, of course. Now, if I could only find his pot of gold.

# How to fold the Leprechaun Hat

◆◇◇◇ LEVEL OF DIFFICULTY

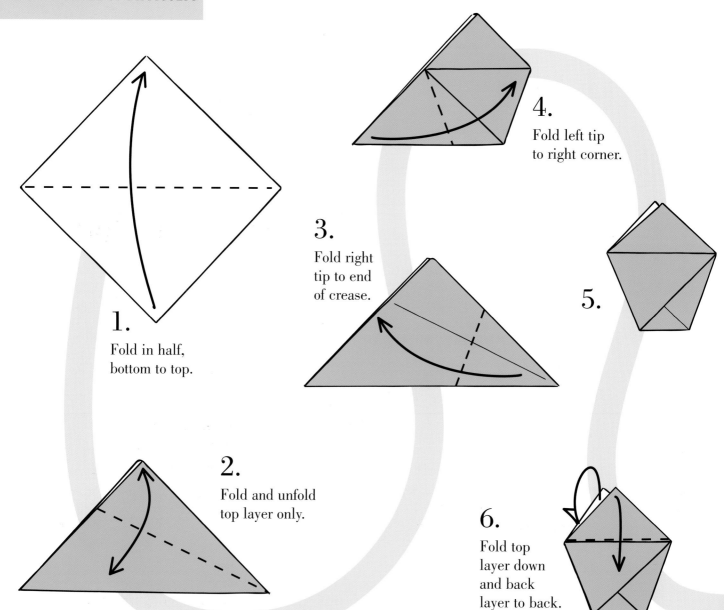

**1.**
Fold in half,
bottom to top.

**2.**
Fold and unfold
top layer only.

**3.**
Fold right
tip to end
of crease.

**4.**
Fold left tip
to right corner.

**5.**

**6.**
Fold top
layer down
and back
layer to back.

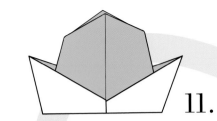

**11.**

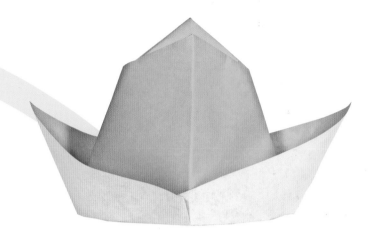

# leprechaun hat

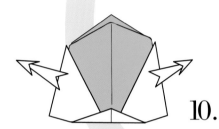

**10.**

Pull flaps to the outside.

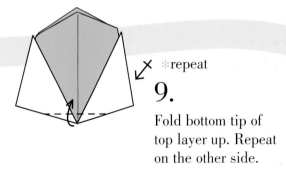

*repeat

**9.**

Fold bottom tip of top layer up. Repeat on the other side.

*rotate

**7.**

You've just made an origami paper cup! If you're thirsty, stop here and pour yourself a drink. Or rotate to continue the leprechaun hat.

*rotate

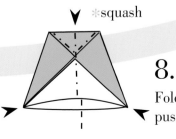

*squash

**8.**

Fold to collapse model, pushing in from the sides.

# betsy's star

*start with an 8½" x 11" sheet, and trim off one inch

Take a piece of printer paper and make a perfect five-pointed star.

◆◇◇◇ LEVEL OF DIFFICULTY

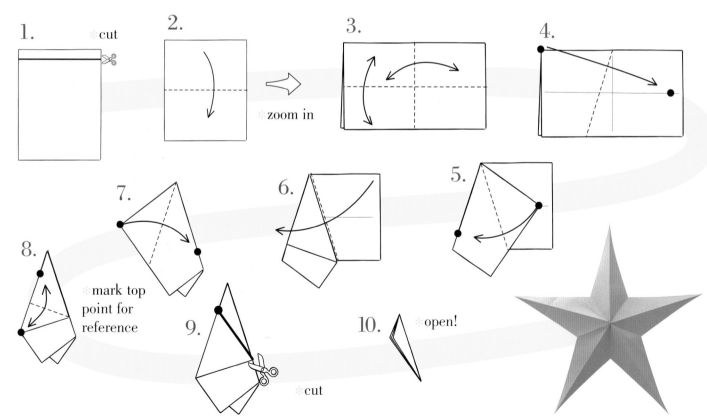

1. *cut

2. *zoom in

3.

4.

5.

6.

7. *mark top point for reference

8.

9. *cut

10. *open!

# easter bunny

Origami is a pleasure any time of year, but origami always makes holidays just a little brighter. For Easter, you need a bunny, of course. (Who else would decorate all those eggs?) Our Easter Bunny is as bright as a basket of jelly beans. Try using him on your Easter egg hunt. He can serve as a directional hint to the location of an egg. And the cute little rascal is so easy to fold. So hop to it! (See you on the bunny trail!)

*Recommended paper*

# HOW TO FOLD THE EASTER BUNNY

◆◇◇◇ LEVEL OF DIFFICULTY

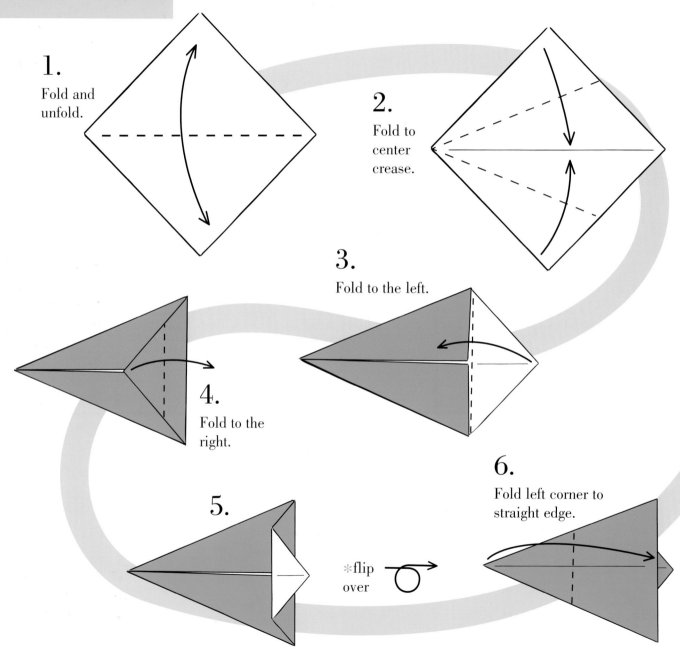

**1.** Fold and unfold.

**2.** Fold to center crease.

**3.** Fold to the left.

**4.** Fold to the right.

**5.**

*flip over

**6.** Fold left corner to straight edge.

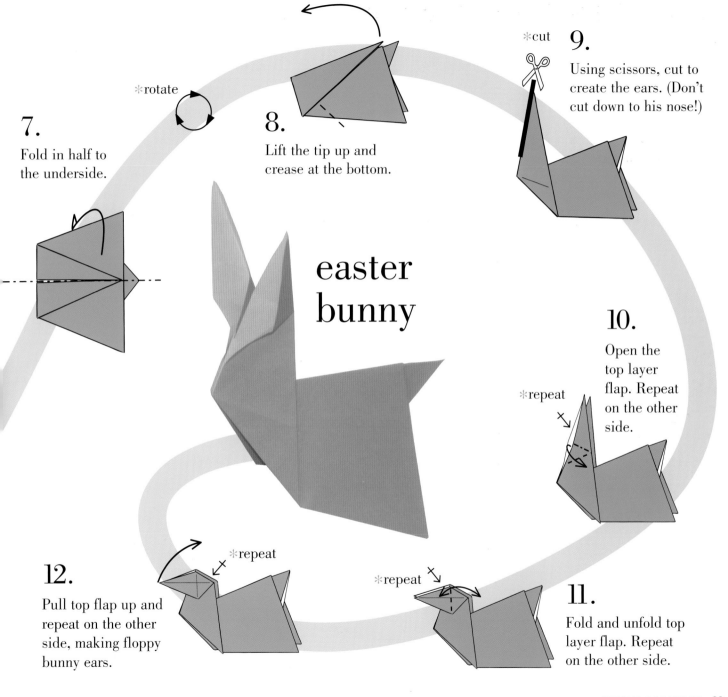

**7.**

Fold in half to the underside.

*rotate

**8.**

Lift the tip up and crease at the bottom.

*cut **9.**

Using scissors, cut to create the ears. (Don't cut down to his nose!)

# easter bunny

**10.**

Open the top layer flap. Repeat on the other side.

*repeat

**12.**

Pull top flap up and repeat on the other side, making floppy bunny ears.

*repeat

*repeat **11.**

Fold and unfold top layer flap. Repeat on the other side.

# dollar viking helmet

You have to hand it to the Norsemen: they made great hats!
Now you can, too.

◆◆◇◇ LEVEL OF DIFFICULTY

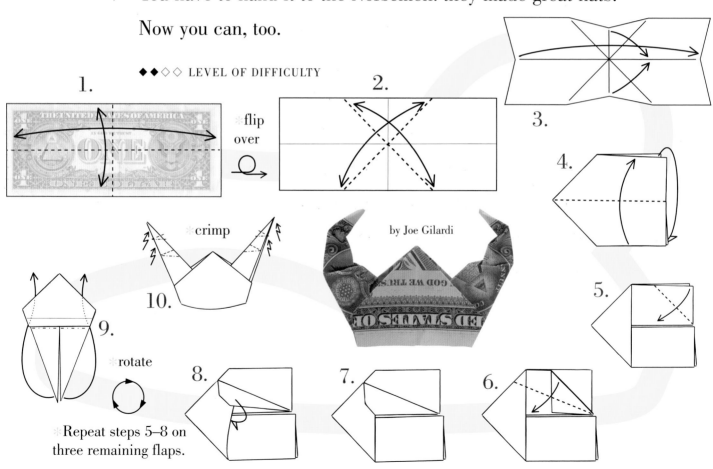

by Joe Gilardi

*flip over

*crimp

*rotate

*Repeat steps 5–8 on three remaining flaps.

# bamboo
# pagoda tower

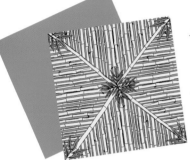

*Recommended paper*

An origami tower is magical. It starts with flat paper, folded into three-dimensional blocks, and, like Jack's beanstalk, can grow and grow and grow. This towering pagoda is based on the architectural icon of ancient Japan. Each level is smaller than the one below and, to build the tower, you'll need to cut the paper to size.

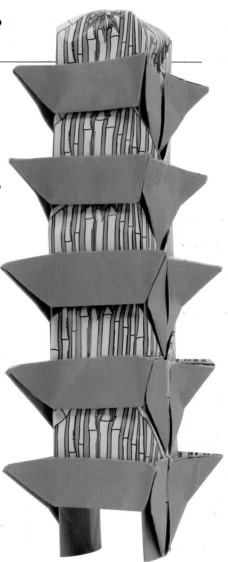

# HOW TO FOLD THE BAMBOO PAGODA TOWER

◆◆◆◇ LEVEL OF DIFFICULTY

**1.**

Fold and unfold.

**2.**

Fold and unfold.

*flip over →

**3.**

Fold and unfold.

**4.**

Collapse model flat following existing creases.

*flip over

**5.**

Look! It's a waterbomb base.

**6.**

Fold the left and right corners of the top layer to the center. Repeat on the other side.

*repeat

**7.**

Squash flap.

*squash

*repeat

**8.**

Flatten.

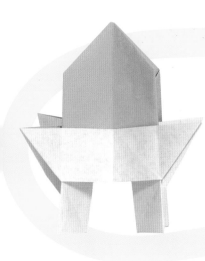

## 17.

Open to make a square base for the pagoda.

## 16.

Open the right flap. Repeat on other side.

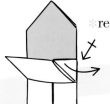

*repeat

## 15.

*repeat

## 13.

Fold and unfold. Repeat on the other side.

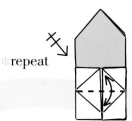

*repeat

## 14.

Open up the left flap. Repeat on the other side.

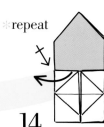

## 12.

Fold the left and right sides of the top layer under. Repeat on the other side.

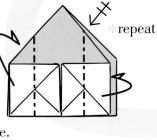

*repeat

## 11.

*repeat

## 9.

Repeat on the other side—open up both flaps.

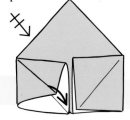

*repeat

## 10.

Fold up the flaps of the top layer. Repeat on the other side.

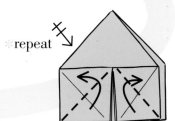

*repeat

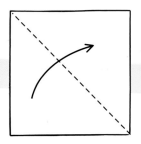

**18.**

Take a new sheet of paper. Fold in half.

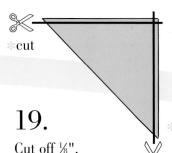

**19.**

Cut off ⅛".

*cut

*cut

**20.**

Repeat steps 1–17.

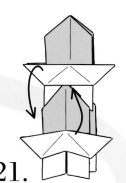

**21.**

Insert the second unit into the first one.

# bamboo pagoda tower

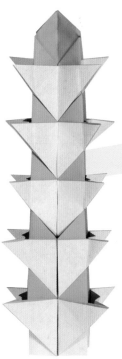

**24.**

Repeat steps 18 and 19. Cut off ½" at step 19. This is the penthouse. Slide it onto the previous units and you're done!

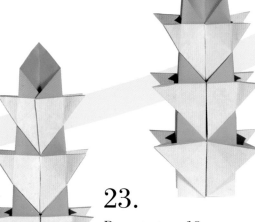

**23.**

Repeat steps 18 and 19. Cut off ⅜" at step 19. Slide the fourth unit onto the third one.

**22.**

Repeat steps 18 and 19. This time, cut off ¼" at step 19. Slide the third unit onto the second one.

# paper dollhouse

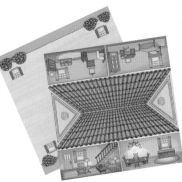

*Recommended paper*

There's something cozy and dear about a little house. The sight can awaken the nine-year-old girl within us all. As you look at the house's walls, one just can't help but imagine the lives of the tiny creatures who reside there. Our Paper Dollhouse makes a great gift, or maybe you'll want to keep it for yourself as a decoration for a coffee table or mantelpiece. Our paper makes a truly one-of-a-kind dwelling.

# How to fold the Paper Doll House

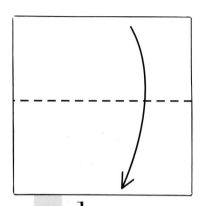

**1.**

Fold in half, top to bottom.

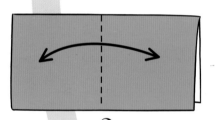

**2.**

Fold and unfold.

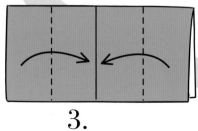

**3.**

Fold left and right to center.

**7.**

Fold left and right to create walls so your house will stand.

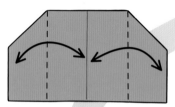

*flip over

## paper doll house

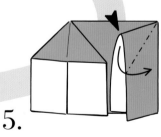

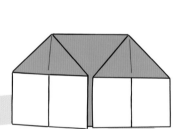

**6.**

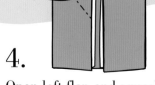

**5.**

Open up and squash.

**4.**

Open left flap and squash.

# Khufu's Great Pyramid

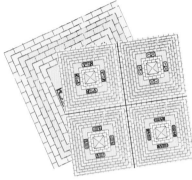

*Recommended paper*

*Cut the paper with the small pyramids into quarters to fold four mini-pyramids.*

Thousands of years ago, an Egyptian geometry nut had a wacky idea. The result was Khufu's Great Pyramid of Giza—the only surviving wonder of the ancient world. Similarly, in modern times, an origami marvel (Anita Barbour by name) looked at a flat, square piece of paper and wondered if it too could be turned into a pyramid. This model may not be one of the world's wonders, but it's still pretty darn nifty. And folding it is a lot less taxing than a trip to Giza to see the real thing.

# How to fold Khufu's Great Pyramid

◆◆◇◇ LEVEL OF DIFFICULTY

**1.**

Fold and unfold.

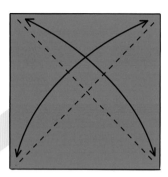

**2.**

Fold all four corners to the center. Crease only in the middle.

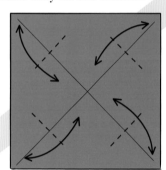

**3.**

Fold all four corners to the creases just made. Crease only in the middle.

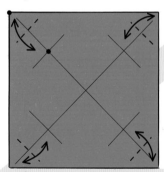

**5.**

Fold all four corners to the crease made in step 4.

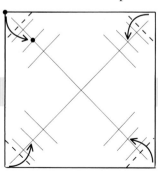

✳flip over

**4.**

Fold so that the two previous creases meet. Crease only in the middle.

*flip over

# khufu's great pyramid

by Anita Barbour

## 9.

Fold each flap in half.

*steps 8 and 9 lock the corners

## 8.

Fold the tips of each corner over to meet its diagonal.

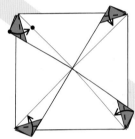

## 6.

Crease the entire fold. Fold and unfold to make diagonals that connect the A Points, B Points, C Points, and D Points.

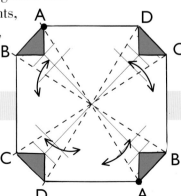

## 7.

Pinch up the four corners along the diagonals. Make the center of the paper concave and flatten paper to one side.

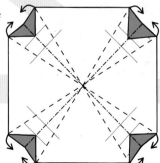

# business reply card chair

Looking for new office decor? Here's another swell model from designer Karen Reeds (see her Business Reply Card Fish, page 66).

◆◆◇◇ LEVEL OF DIFFICULTY

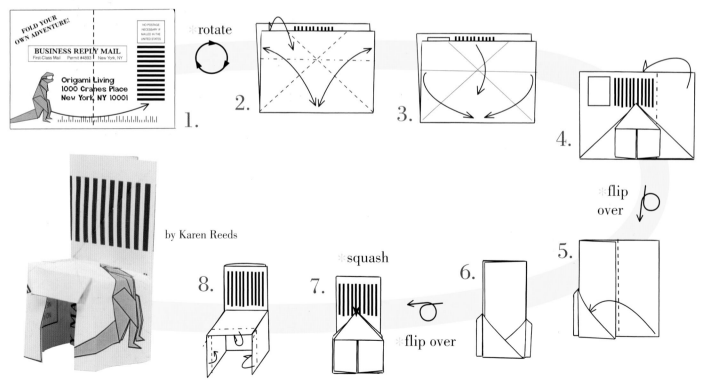

by Karen Reeds

# good luck fish

Know someone who could use some good luck? Maybe his or her lucky penny, shamrock, or rabbit's foot has lost its mojo. Turn to origami. The sea bream (known as *tai* in Japanese) is a symbol of good fortune, wealth, and prosperity. All in all, it's a great fish to have around the house. And the wide-mouth model is one of the cutest origami fish around (if you look closely at our paper, you'll see the scales are actually lucky horseshoes).

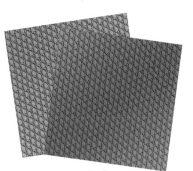

*Recommended paper*

# How to fold the Good Luck Fish

◆◆◇◇ LEVEL OF DIFFICULTY

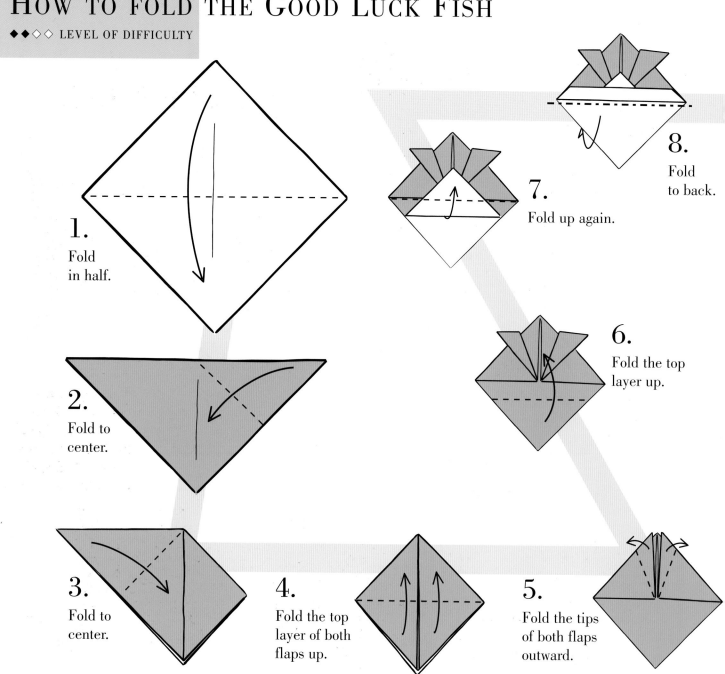

**1.** Fold in half.

**2.** Fold to center.

**3.** Fold to center.

**4.** Fold the top layer of both flaps up.

**5.** Fold the tips of both flaps outward.

**6.** Fold the top layer up.

**7.** Fold up again.

**8.** Fold to back.

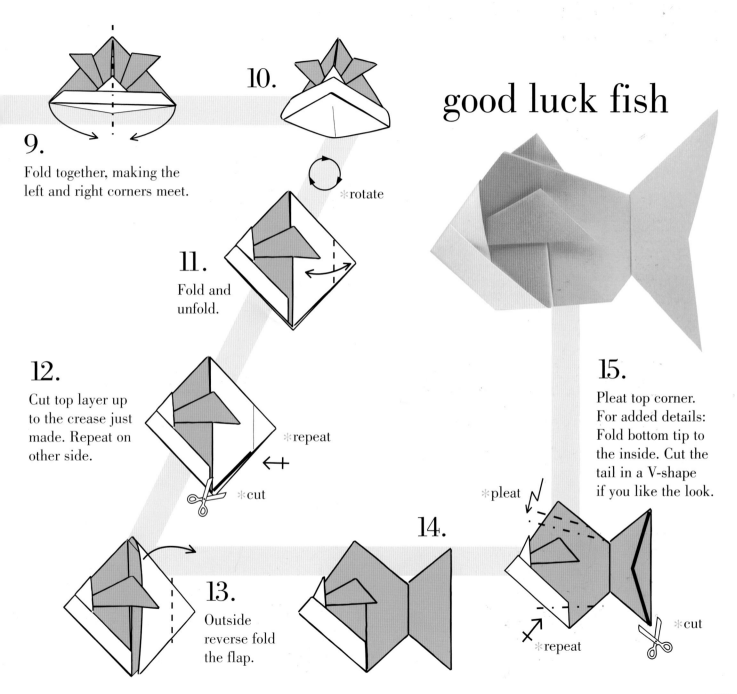

**9.**
Fold together, making the left and right corners meet.

**10.**

✳rotate

# good luck fish

**11.**
Fold and unfold.

**12.**
Cut top layer up to the crease just made. Repeat on other side.

✳repeat

✳cut

**13.**
Outside reverse fold the flap.

**14.**

**15.**
Pleat top corner. For added details: Fold bottom tip to the inside. Cut the tail in a V-shape if you like the look.

✳pleat

✳repeat

✳cut

# paper
# book

Start with a piece of 8½" x 11" printer paper (what we used to call typing paper) and make yourself a book.

◆◇◇◇ LEVEL OF DIFFICULTY

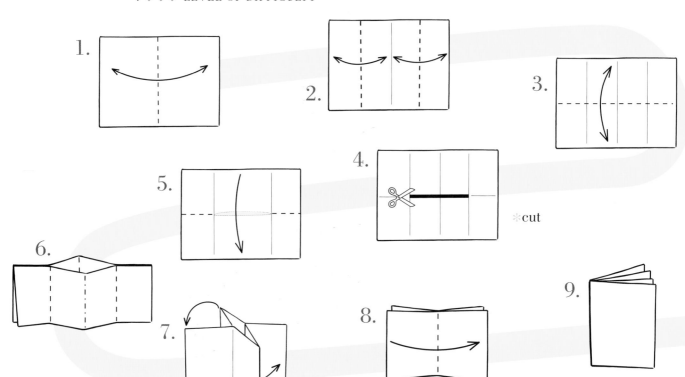

# rabbit of wisdom

In folklore around the world, the rabbit is always a smart cookie. Constantly in danger from stronger foes, he uses his wits to escape them. There are many origami rabbits, but there is only one Rabbit of Wisdom (and he looks darn cute with an origami book). Make the pair to tickle the fancy of a smart friend!

*Recommended paper*

# HOW TO FOLD THE RABBIT OF WISDOM

◆◆◇◇ LEVEL OF DIFFICULTY

**5.**

Open and
fold at the
same time.

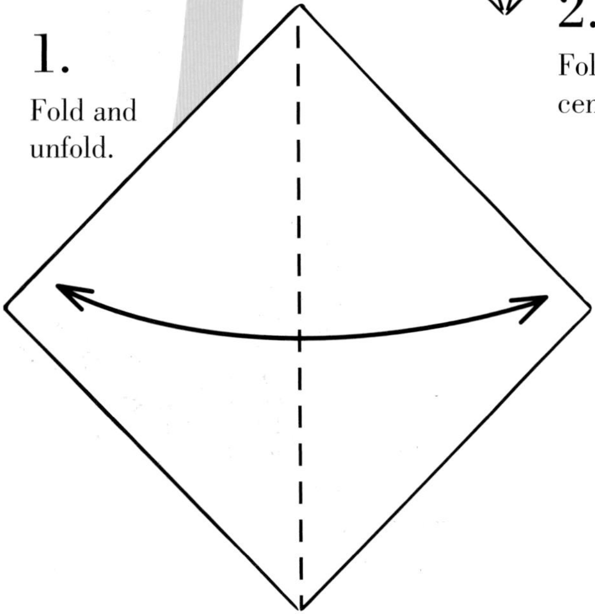

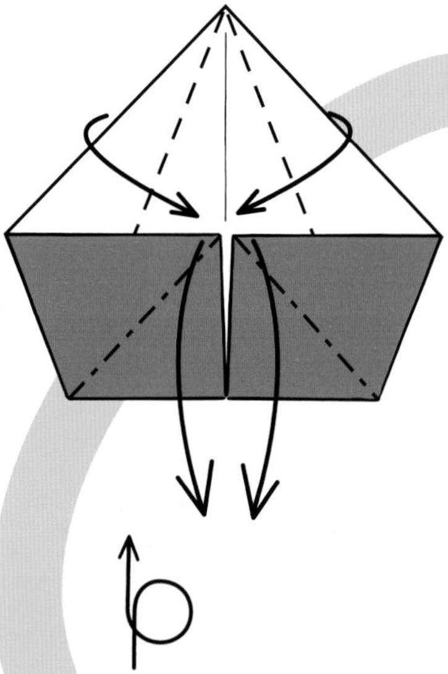

*flip over

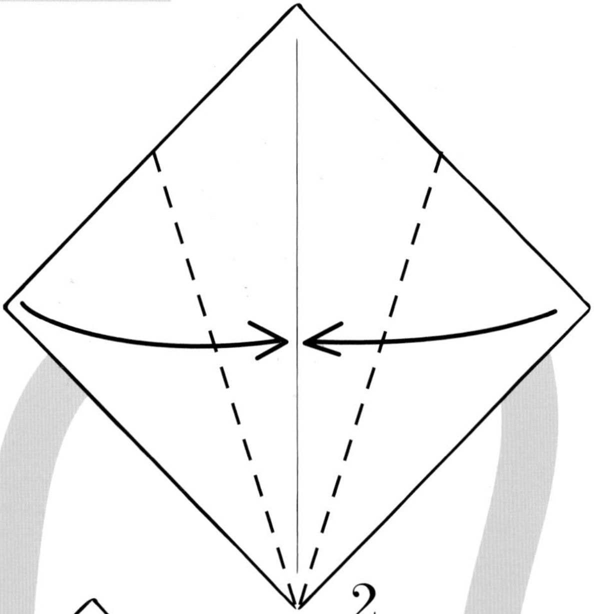

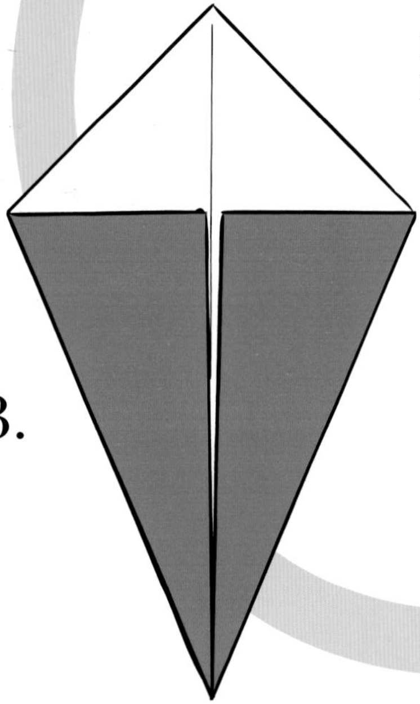

**2.**

Fold to
center.

**1.**

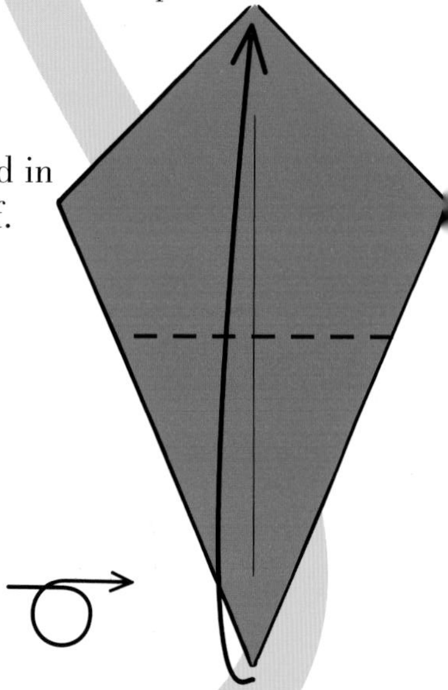

Fold and
unfold.

**4.**

Fold in
half.

**3.**

*flip over

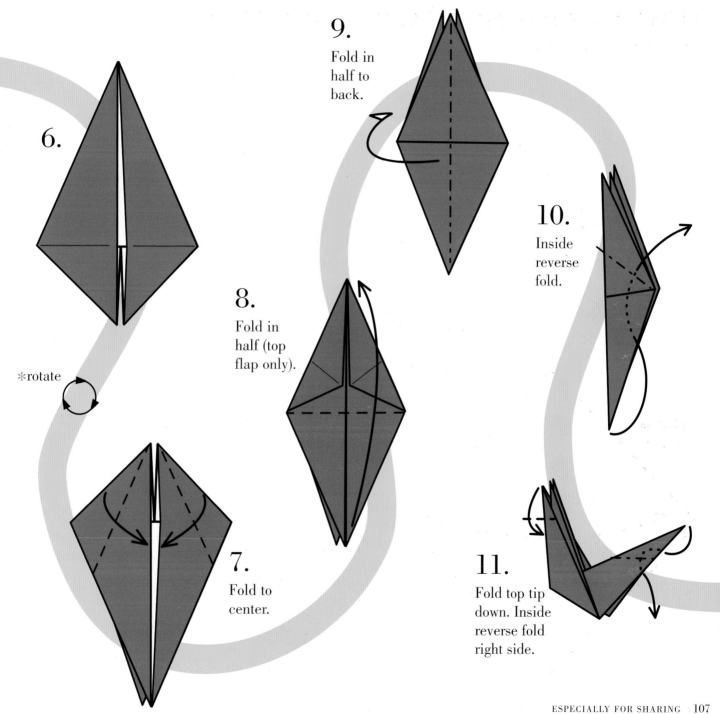

**6.**

*rotate

**7.**

Fold to
center.

**8.**

Fold in
half (top
flap only).

**9.**

Fold in
half to
back.

**10.**

Inside
reverse
fold.

**11.**

Fold top tip
down. Inside
reverse fold
right side.

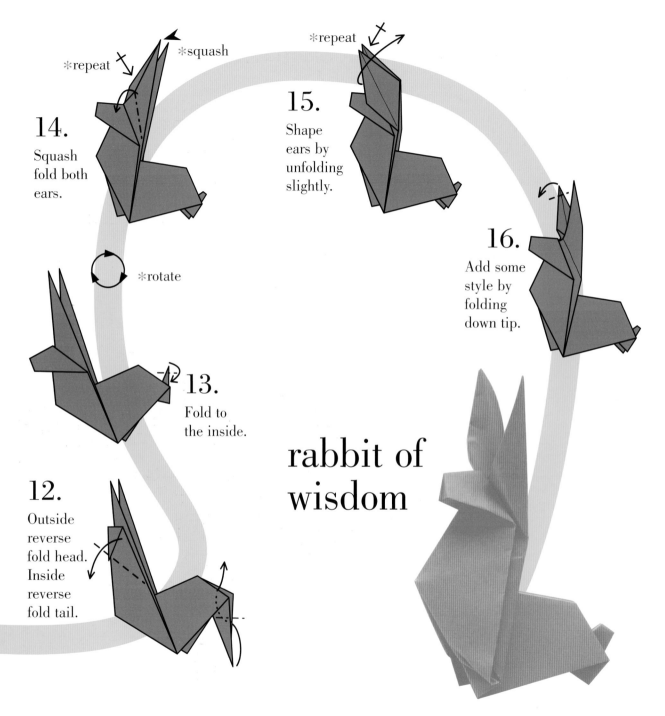

**14.**

Squash fold both ears.

*repeat

*squash

**15.**

Shape ears by unfolding slightly.

*repeat

**16.**

Add some style by folding down tip.

*rotate

**13.**

Fold to the inside.

# rabbit of wisdom

**12.**

Outside reverse fold head. Inside reverse fold tail.

# ninja star

The power of the ninja is with you! This wonderful *shuriken,* the Ninja Star, is a two-part model that locks together. But no throwing in the house or at anyone! This star is very sturdy and will really fly. (No kidding!) Our paper lends a cosmic touch to this decorative weapon from Japan.

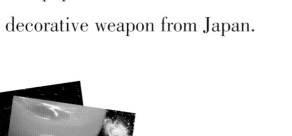

*Recommended paper*

# How to fold the Ninja Star

◆◆◇◇ LEVEL OF DIFFICULTY

## 1.
Fold and unfold.

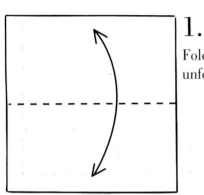

## 2.
Fold top and bottom to the crease.

## 3.
Fold in half, bottom to top.

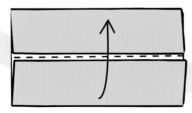

## 4.
Fold and unfold.

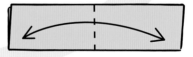

## 5.
Fold the corners to the edges.

## 6.
Fold the right corner down.

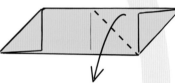

## 7.
Fold the left corner up. This is the first part of the model, part **A**.

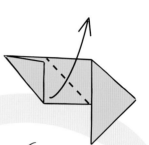

## 8.
Take a new sheet of paper to fold the second part of the model.

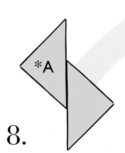

*A

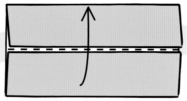

**3.**

Fold in half,
bottom to top.

**2.**

Fold top
and bottom
to the crease.

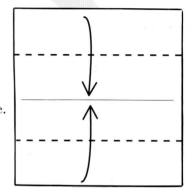

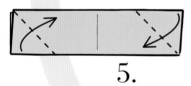

**4.**

Fold and
unfold.

**1.**

Fold and unfold, part **B**.

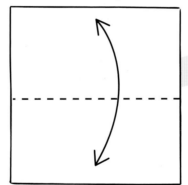

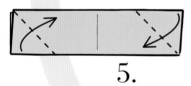

**5.**

Fold the corners
to the edges.

**6.**

Fold the right
corner up.

**7.**

Fold the left
corner down.

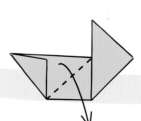

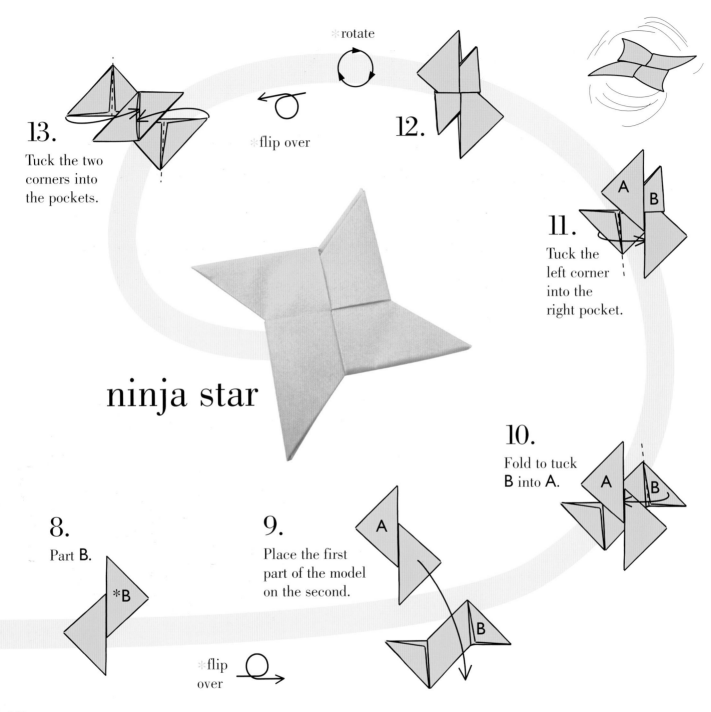

**13.**
Tuck the two corners into the pockets.

*rotate

*flip over

**12.**

**11.**
Tuck the left corner into the right pocket.

A  B

**10.**
Fold to tuck B into A.

A  B

ninja star

**8.**
Part **B**.

*B

**9.**
Place the first part of the model on the second.

A

B

*flip over

# surprise box

*Recommended paper*

Origami guru Gay Merrill Gross first became hooked on origami when she unfolded a napkin in a restaurant and was intrigued by the creases the folds had made. Her Surprise Box (a box-within-a-box) is a lovely way to give a gift. Just don't be surprised if the recipient likes the package as much as what's inside.

# How to fold the Surprise Box

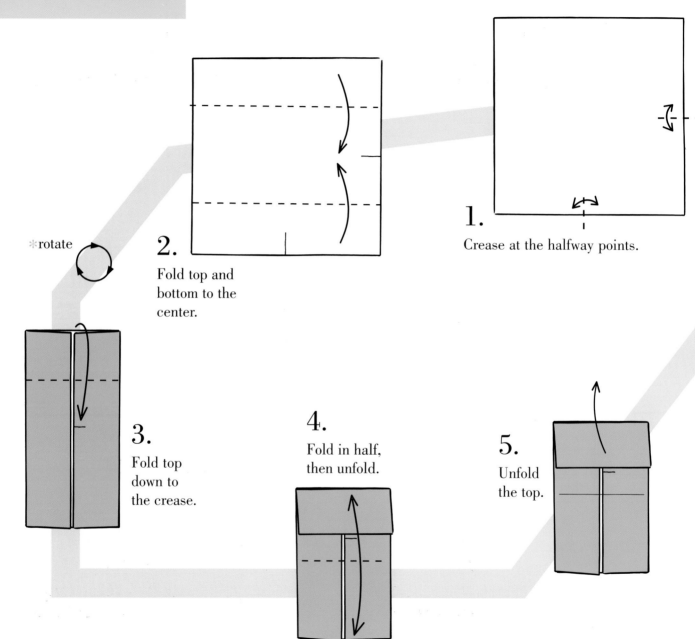

**1.** Crease at the halfway points.

*rotate

**2.** Fold top and bottom to the center.

**3.** Fold top down to the crease.

**4.** Fold in half, then unfold.

**5.** Unfold the top.

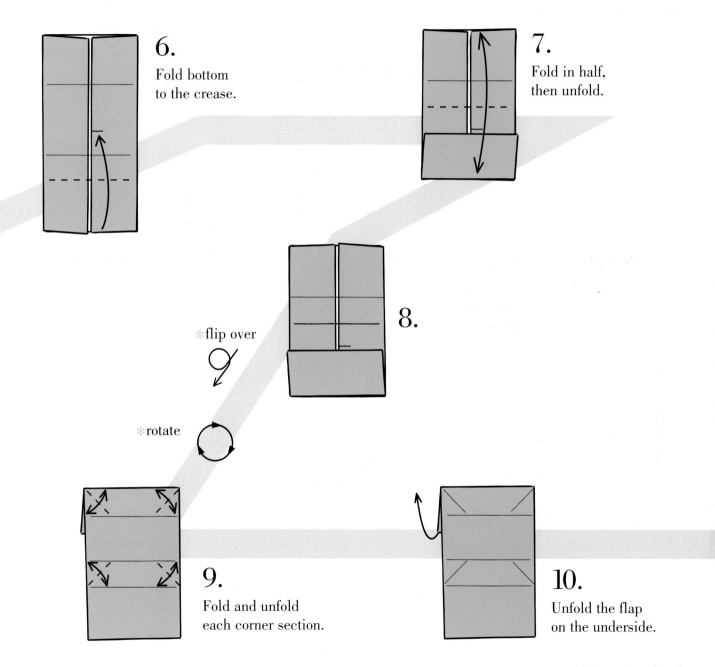

**6.**
Fold bottom
to the crease.

**7.**
Fold in half,
then unfold.

**8.**

*flip over

*rotate

**9.**
Fold and unfold
each corner section.

**10.**
Unfold the flap
on the underside.

**13.**

Reverse fold top and
bottom edges of right-
hand side slightly.

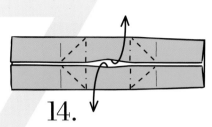

**14.**

Crease the folds open
in the center while
raising the side panels.

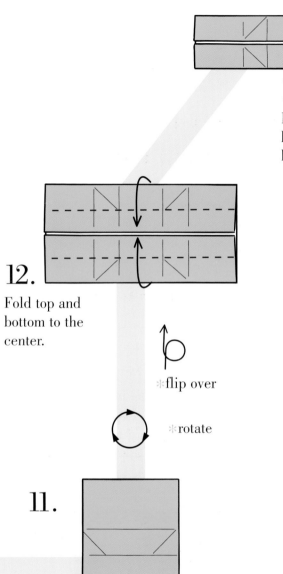

**12.**

Fold top and
bottom to the
center.

✳flip over

✳rotate

**11.**

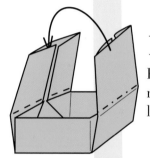

**15.**

Fold to tuck
right flap into
left pocket.

# surprise box

by Gay Merrill Gross

# wildflower box

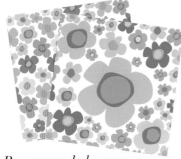

*Recommended paper*

Let's hear it for wild beauty! It makes the world a more colorful place. Wildflowers are nature's free spirits, popping up wherever they choose, adding bursts of color to meadows and roadsides. To pay tribute to these wild-and-crazy blossoms, we offer this Wildflower Box. Use it to tame the loose, runaway items in your desk drawer or pass it on as a gift.

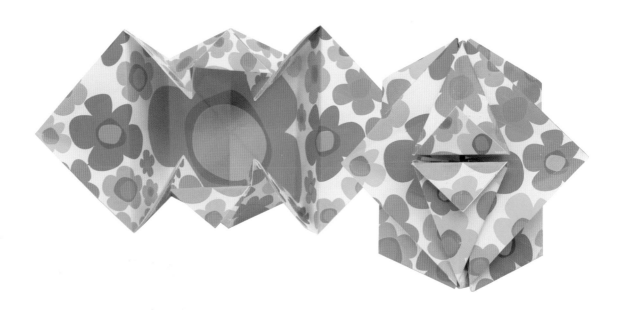

# HOW TO FOLD THE WILDFLOWER BOX

◆◆◆◇ LEVEL OF DIFFICULTY

**2.**

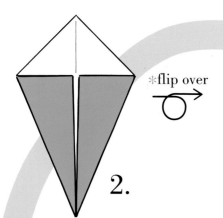

*flip over

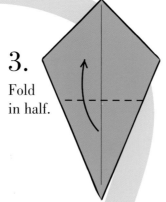

**3.**

Fold
in half.

*flip over

**1.**

First, fold the paper in
half and unfold. Second,
fold left and right to center
crease.

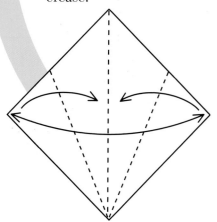

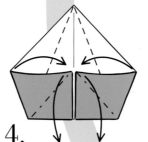

**4.**

Open and
fold in at the
same time.

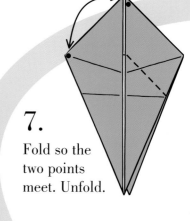

**7.**

Fold so the
two points
meet. Unfold.

*repeat

**6.**

Fold and unfold
the top layer up.
Repeat on the
other side.

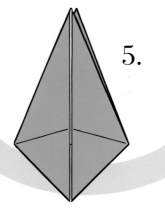

**5.**

*rotate

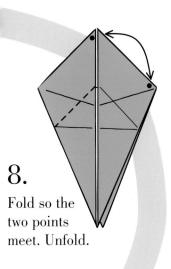

## 8.

Fold so the two points meet. Unfold.

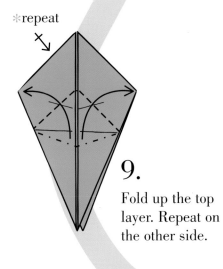

*repeat

## 9.

Fold up the top layer. Repeat on the other side.

## 10.

Fold the top layer up.

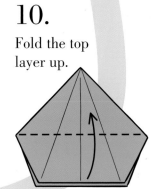

## 11.

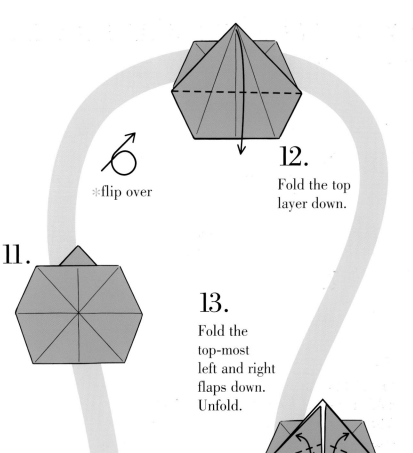

*flip over

## 12.

Fold the top layer down.

## 13.

Fold the top-most left and right flaps down. Unfold.

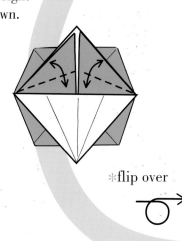

*flip over

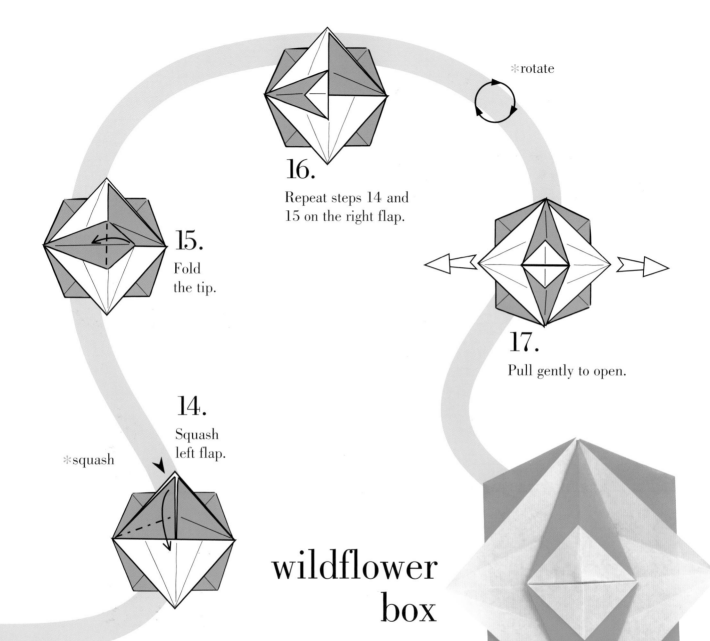

**16.**

Repeat steps 14 and 15 on the right flap.

*rotate

**15.**

Fold the tip.

**17.**

Pull gently to open.

**14.**

Squash left flap.

*squash

# wildflower box

# lighthouse bookmark

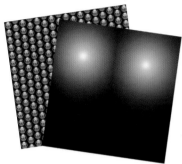

*Recommended paper*

A person can never have too many books—or bookmarks. For years, I used anything that was handy: bank statements, sticky notes, pencils . . . but then, I started folding my own bookmarks. This model is in the symbolically significant shape of a lighthouse; it will guide you to your place. Give one to your favorite librarian or book lover. Or use regular origami paper and fold a batch and give them away at the next community sale at your local library.

# How to fold the Lighthouse Bookmark

◆◆◆◇ LEVEL OF DIFFICULTY

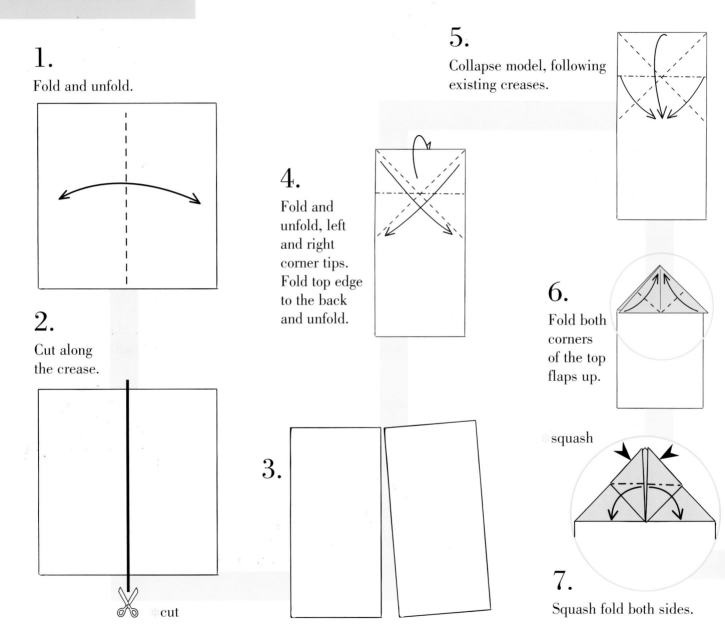

### 1.
Fold and unfold.

### 2.
Cut along the crease.

✂ *cut

### 3.

### 4.
Fold and unfold, left and right corner tips. Fold top edge to the back and unfold.

### 5.
Collapse model, following existing creases.

### 6.
Fold both corners of the top flaps up.

*squash

### 7.
Squash fold both sides.

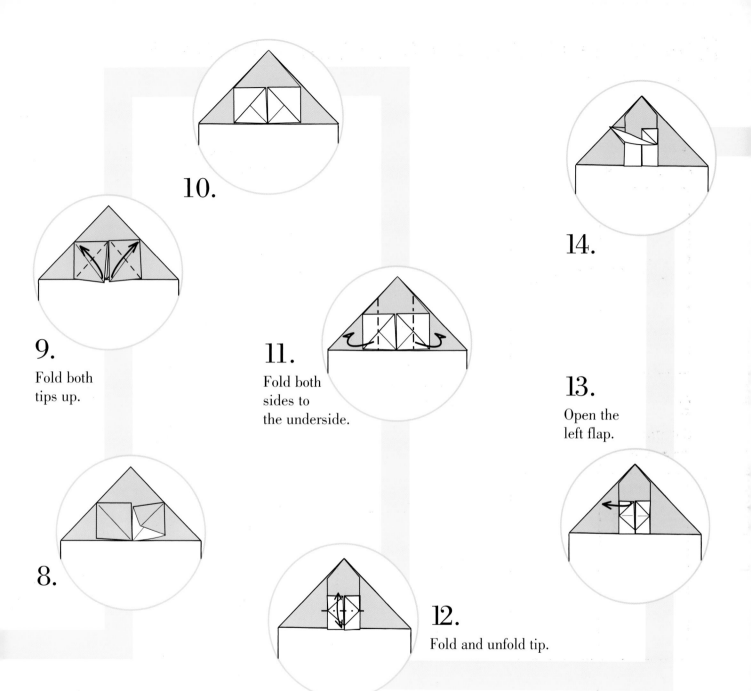

**10.**

**9.**
Fold both
tips up.

**11.**
Fold both
sides to
the underside.

**8.**

**12.**
Fold and unfold tip.

**14.**

**13.**
Open the
left flap.

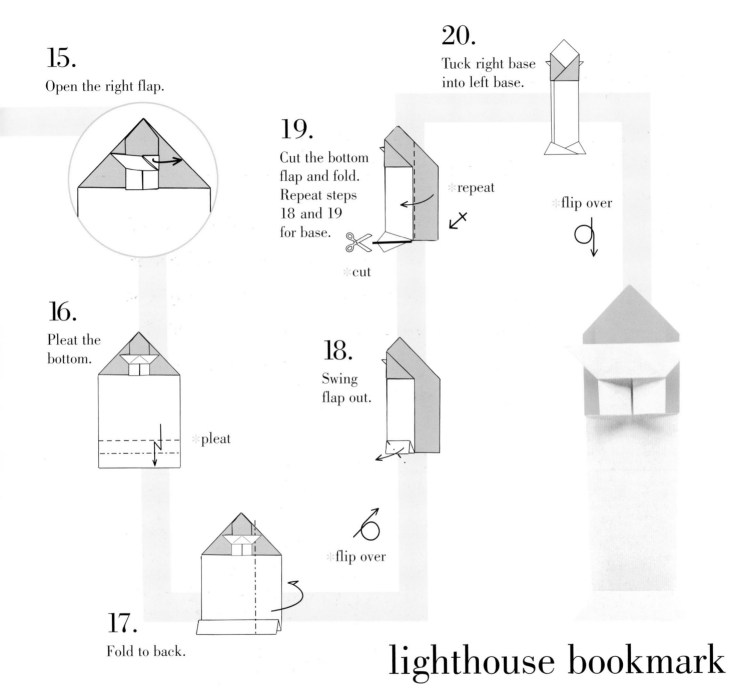

## 15.

Open the right flap.

## 16.

Pleat the bottom.

*pleat

## 17.

Fold to back.

*flip over

## 18.

Swing flap out.

## 19.

Cut the bottom flap and fold. Repeat steps 18 and 19 for base.

*cut

*repeat

## 20.

Tuck right base into left base.

*flip over

# lighthouse bookmark

# pop-up greeting card

*Recommended paper*

Sure, e-mail is fast, but nothing beats the impact of a card delivered by the United States Postal Service. Our Pop-Up Greeting Card is a smashing way to say thanks, congratulations, or just stay in touch! The artwork inside pops out to be four times the size of the card itself.

# How to fold the Pop-Up Greeting Card

◆◆◇◇ LEVEL OF DIFFICULTY

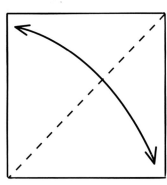

**1.**

Fold and unfold.

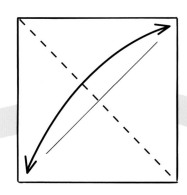

**2.**

Fold and unfold.

 *flip over

*flip over

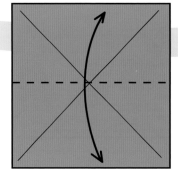

**3.**

Fold and unfold.

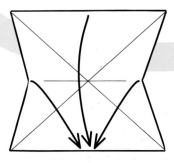

**4.**

Collapse model flat following existing creases.

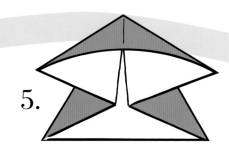

**5.**

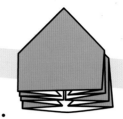

**11.**

*repeat

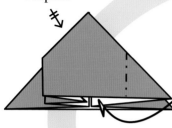

**10.**

Inside reverse fold on right flap, top layer only. Repeat on other side.

**9.**

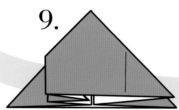

**8.**

Inside reverse fold on left flap, top layer only.

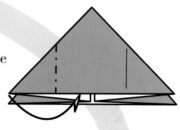

**6.**

Look! It's a waterbomb base.

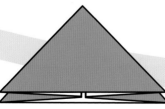

**7.**

Fold and unfold left and right corners to center of bottom edge. Repeat on the other side.

*repeat

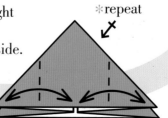

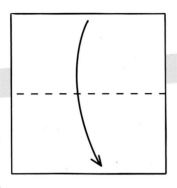

## 12.

Fold a new sheet of paper in half.

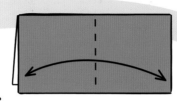

## 13.

Fold in half, then unfold.

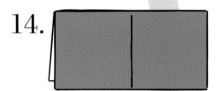

## 14.

# pop-up greeting card

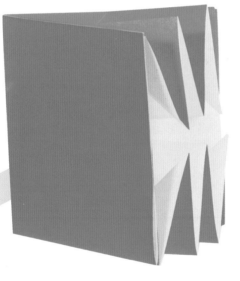

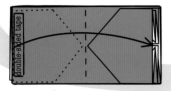

## 15.

Add double-sided tape along the left and right edges.

## 17.

Fold the left side over the right to close card.

## 16.

Place the first sheet of paper over the tape, as indicated by dots.

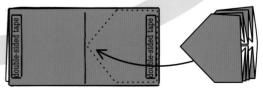

# tyrannosaurus rex

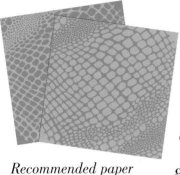

*Recommended paper*

Hail, King of the Dinosaurs! This T. Rex model is by origami model master, Kunihiko Kasahara. It's one of my favorite paper dinos because of its lovely bits of detail. (Don't you just love the tail?) This is a perfect gift for the dinosaur-crazy kids in your life.

But beware. Once you make it, you may like it so much that you won't be able to part with it. So c'mon, let me hear it: RRRRRRRAWWWWWWWRRRRGGGGHHHHHH!

# HOW TO FOLD THE TYRANNOSAURUS REX

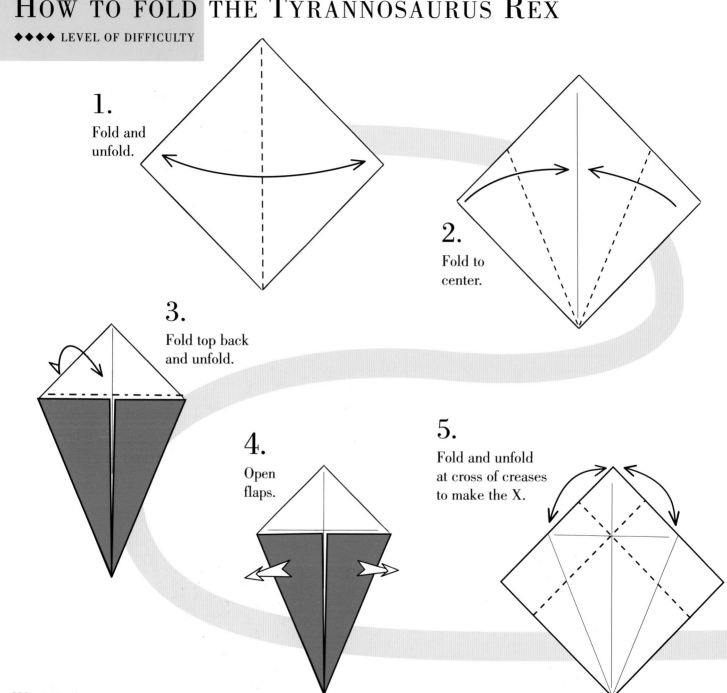

**1.**
Fold and unfold.

**2.**
Fold to center.

**3.**
Fold top back and unfold.

**4.**
Open flaps.

**5.**
Fold and unfold at cross of creases to make the X.

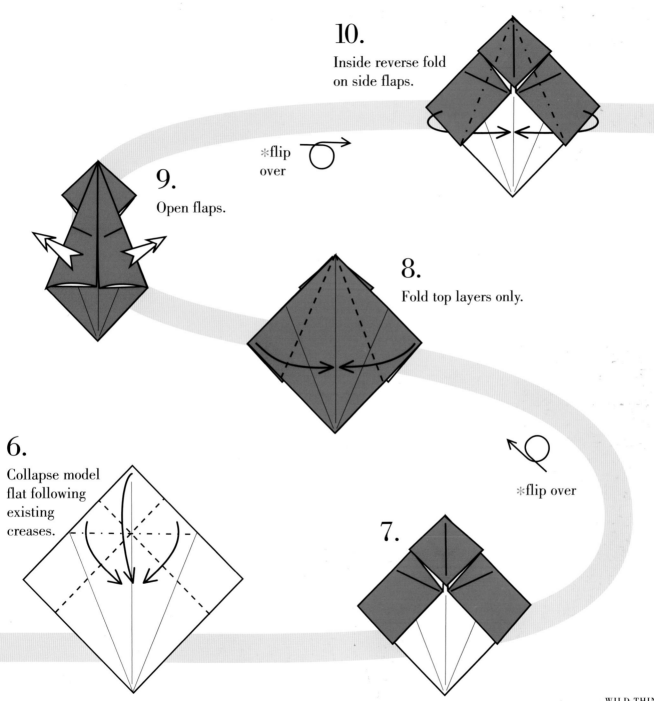

**10.**

Inside reverse fold on side flaps.

*flip over

**9.**

Open flaps.

**8.**

Fold top layers only.

**6.**

Collapse model flat following existing creases.

*flip over

**7.**

## 11.

Fold bottom layer
under top layer.

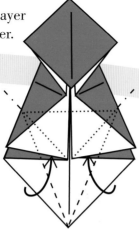

## 12.

Open right
flap and
flatten to
center.

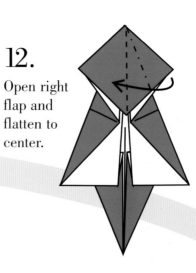

## 13.

Raise to fold left and right corners
up and in, to meet in center.

## 14.

Repeat steps 12
and 13 on left flap.

## 15.

Fold top
layer left.

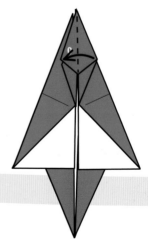

## 19.

Fold the inner top tip down. Fold in half to the back.

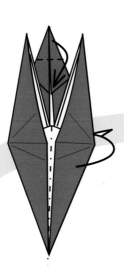

## 20.

Fold the lower edge in and the top layer out. Repeat on other side.

*repeat

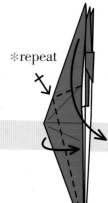

## 18.

Repeat steps 16 and 17 on right side.

## 16.

Fold the tip of the top section up. Fold left side to raise tip to the top.

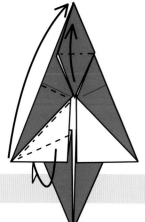

## 17.

Gently press edges into center.

## 21.

To create the head, outside reverse the forehead and jaw. Inside reverse fold to create the tail. Inside reverse the thigh areas on both sides.

*repeat

## 22.

To create teeth, inside reverse both tips a little. Inside reverse both legs to create calves.

*repeat

# tyrannosaurus rex

by Kunihiko Kasahara

## 23.

Fold the tail in and out. Inside reverse fold the bottom tips of each leg to make feet. To create arms, make the three creases shown, pinching each tip up and out to the sides.

*repeat

*repeat

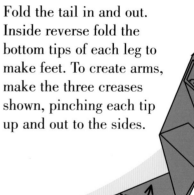

# jumping
# leopard frog

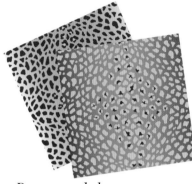

*Recommended paper*
*Cut the paper into quarters*
*to make four little leapers.*

This model is perhaps the best of all for sharing. No one can resist this cute jumping frog. It is my favorite to teach because it's easy to fold, jumps quite nicely, and can safely travel in your pocket. The paper we've designed has a leopard frog pattern (yes, there is such a thing) to make this guy even more irresistible. Of course, there's another reason this model is ideal to share: origami competition! Challenge your friends to a jumping contest (this is great fun with a group of kids) and see whose hopper can leap the highest. You can also make a dandy jumping frog from a business card. Just start from step 2.

# HOW TO FOLD THE JUMPING LEOPARD FROG

◆◆◇◇ LEVEL OF DIFFICULTY

**3.**

Fold top half to center crease and unfold.

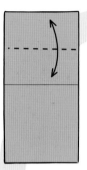

*flip over

**2.**

Fold and unfold.

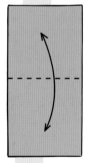

**1.**

Fold in half.

**4.**

Fold to make diagonals and unfold.

# jumping leopard frog

With a finger, make a quick downward stroke here.

**★**

**5.**

Collapse model flat following existing creases.

**9.**

Fold bottom edge to the underside, then fold top portion up.

**8.**

Fold both sides to center. Fold top flaps out.

**7.**

Fold both tips of top layer up.

**6.**

Fold bottom edge up.

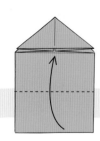

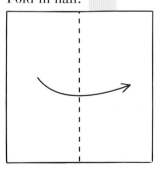

# foxy puppet

*Recommended paper*

Do you enjoy speaking in a funny voice and having kids think you're the coolest thing on earth? Fold the Foxy Puppet. It's versatile, too. It can sing along with your favorite tunes, or mimic an annoying lecture. Perhaps you'll discover a new career as a ventriloquist (just don't forget that you owe it all to origami). The possibilities are endless with this foxy fellow on hand.

# How to fold the Foxy Puppet

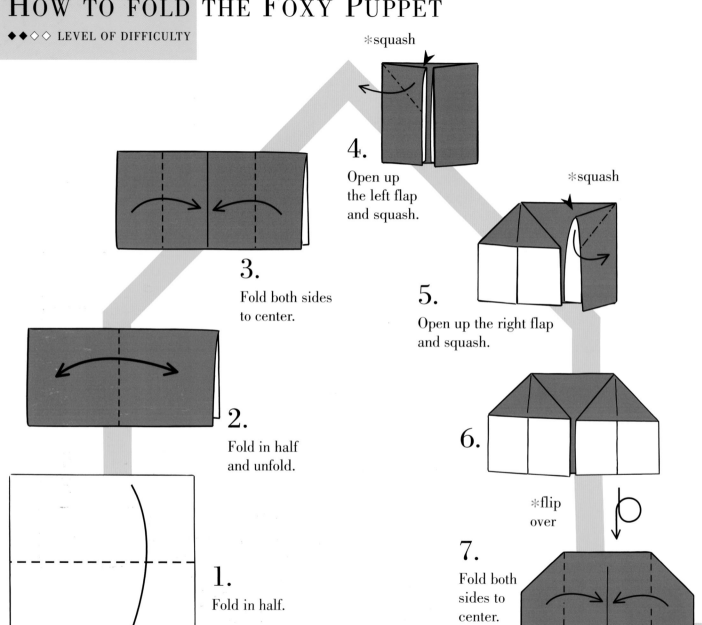

*squash

**4.**

Open up
the left flap
and squash.

*squash

**3.**

Fold both sides
to center.

**5.**

Open up the right flap
and squash.

**2.**

Fold in half
and unfold.

**6.**

*flip
over

**7.**

Fold both
sides to
center.

**1.**

Fold in half.

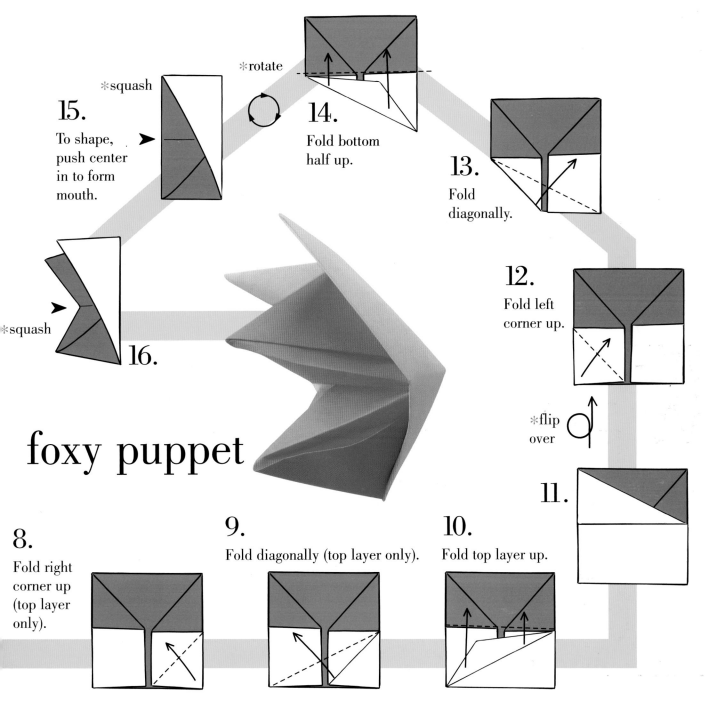

**15.**
*squash

To shape, push center in to form mouth.

*rotate

**14.**
Fold bottom half up.

**13.**
Fold diagonally.

**12.**
Fold left corner up.

*flip over

**11.**

*squash

**16.**

# foxy puppet

**8.**
Fold right corner up (top layer only).

**9.**
Fold diagonally (top layer only).

**10.**
Fold top layer up.

# two-dollar pantsuit

You'll need two dollars for this model, but you'll end up looking like a million bucks!

◆ ◇ ◇ ◇ LEVEL OF DIFFICULTY

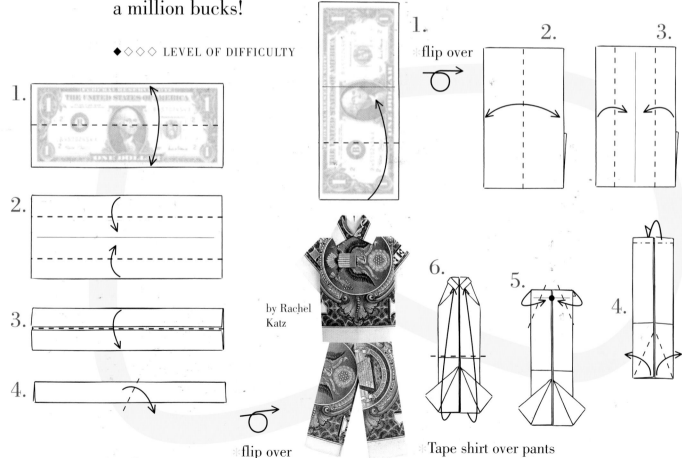

1.

2.

3.

4.

1. flip over

2.

3.

6.

5.

4.

by Rachel Katz

flip over

Tape shirt over pants

# inflatable goldfish

*Recommended paper*

The Inflatable Goldfish is just a little more challenging than our one-star models, and it's a good one to raise your origami skills up a notch. The model is dandy because its triangular body looks good from all sides. In fact, if you're craftily inclined, you could use the Inflatable Goldfish on an origami mobile (along with the Good Luck Fish, see page 101). Whether it's hanging in the air or used as a desk decoration, this fish is a guaranteed room brightener.

# How to fold the Inflatable Goldfish

**1.**
Fold and unfold.

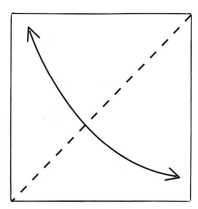

**2.**
Fold and unfold.

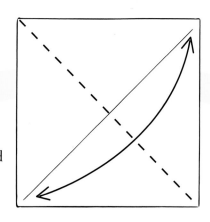

*flip over

**3.**
Fold and unfold.

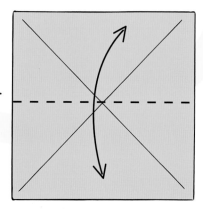

**4.**
Collapse model flat following existing creases.

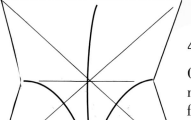

*flip over

**5.**
Look! It's a waterbomb base.

**6.**
Fold both tips of top layer up.

**7.**
Fold both corners to center.

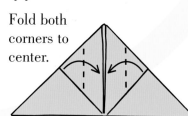

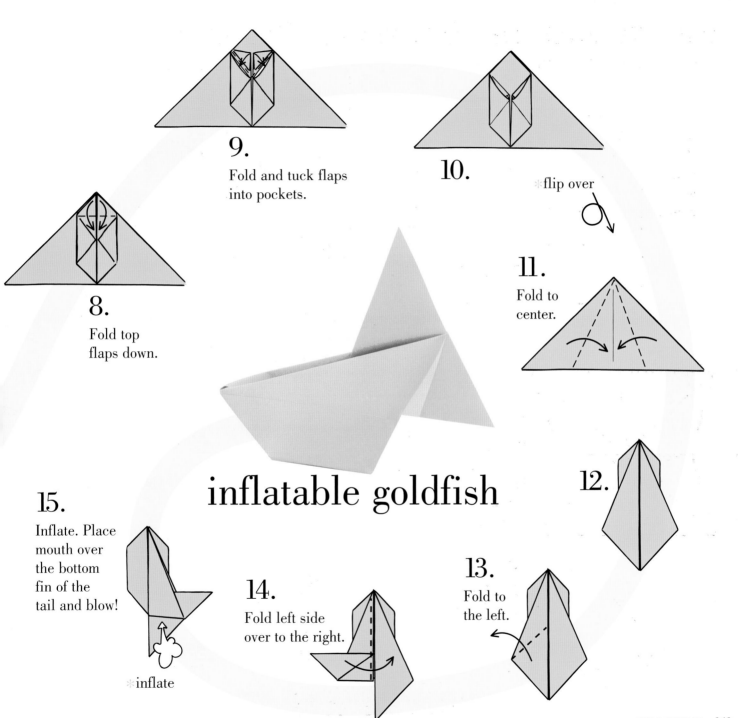

**9.**
Fold and tuck flaps into pockets.

**10.**

❋ flip over

**8.**
Fold top flaps down.

**11.**
Fold to center.

**12.**

**inflatable goldfish**

**15.**
Inflate. Place mouth over the bottom fin of the tail and blow!

❋ inflate

**14.**
Fold left side over to the right.

**13.**
Fold to the left.

# origami
# swami turban

With a sheet of printer paper, you can become an Origami Swami.

Dispense the wisdom of folding to one and all!

◆◇◇◇ LEVEL OF DIFFICULTY

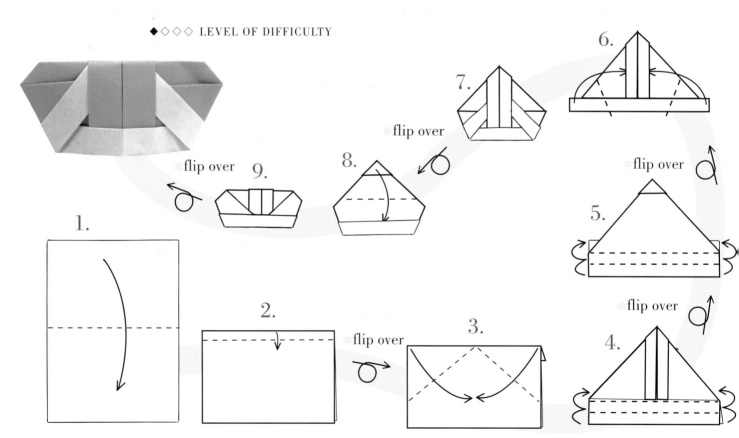

# one-trick pony

*Recommended paper*

Always wanted a pony but never got to have one? Well, your ponyless days are a thing of the past. As an added bonus, this model is a special pony because it can do a trick. Place the finished model on a tabletop. Put your index finger under its tail and give it a flick upward. The pony will flip over in the air and land on its feet—executing a 360-degree circle. Ta-daaa! Like any trick, it will take some practice. But imagine your pride in being the proud owner of a One-Trick Pony (don't forget the sugar cubes for rewards).

Artwork © Robert Zimmerman

# How to fold the One-Trick Pony

◆◆◇◇ LEVEL OF DIFFICULTY

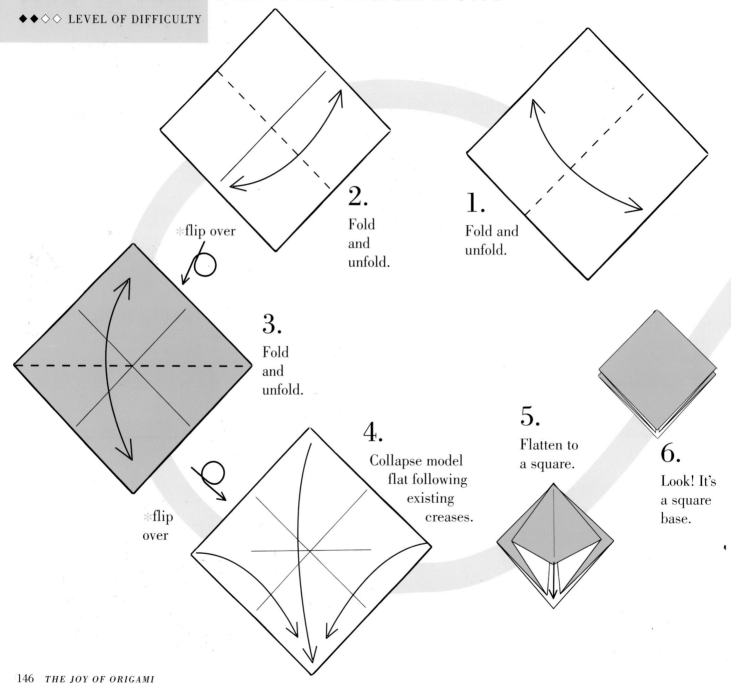

**2.** Fold and unfold.

**1.** Fold and unfold.

*flip over

**3.** Fold and unfold.

*flip over

**4.** Collapse model flat following existing creases.

**5.** Flatten to a square.

**6.** Look! It's a square base.

## 7.
Fold both corners of top layer to center, then fold top down. Repeat on other side. Unfold paper.

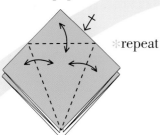

## 8.
Cut top and bottom to the square.

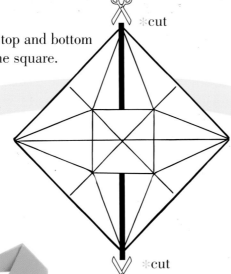

## 9.
Refold paper into square base. Fold both flaps of top layer up. Repeat on other side.

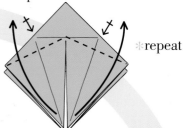

## one-trick pony

This pony will flip 360°. Flick up its tail and it will land on its hooves.

## 10.
Fold both tips down. Repeat on other side.

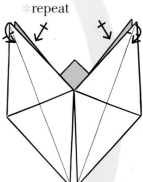

## 11.
Fold both sides to the center. Repeat on other side.

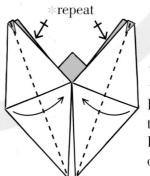

*rotate

## 12.
Inside reverse fold to make head. Inside reverse fold to make tail.

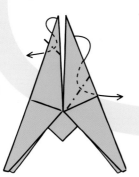

# sunrise napkin

Pleat-fold a napkin to brighten your table!

◆◆◇◇ LEVEL OF DIFFICULTY

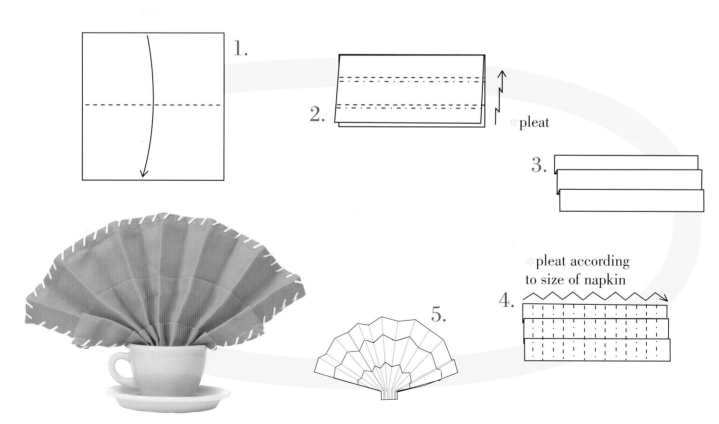

1.

2. *pleat

3.

4. *pleat according to size of napkin

5.

# elephant
# in pajamas

You may remember that old Groucho Marx joke: "This morning I shot an elephant in my pajamas. How he got in my pajamas I'll never know." (Wacka, wacka!) But seriously, folks . . . Maybe it's time for Mr. Elephant to have a pair of PJs of his own. And I think he'd choose our striped patterns if only he could. This is a fun model for kids to fold, or for the young at heart—and who isn't with an Elephant in Pajamas in their hands?

*Recommended paper*

# HOW TO FOLD THE ELEPHANT IN PAJAMAS

◆◇◇◇ LEVEL OF DIFFICULTY

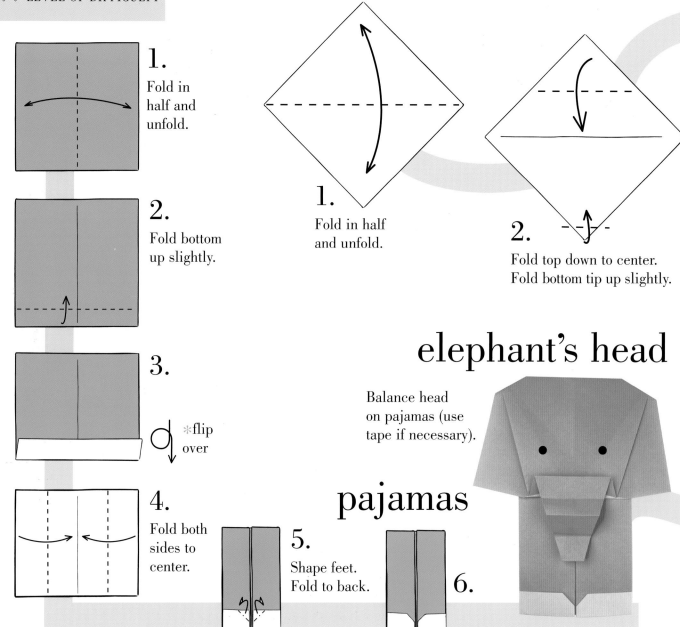

**1.**
Fold in half and unfold.

**2.**
Fold bottom up slightly.

**3.**
✳flip over

**4.**
Fold both sides to center.

**1.**
Fold in half and unfold.

**2.**
Fold top down to center. Fold bottom tip up slightly.

## elephant's head

Balance head on pajamas (use tape if necessary).

## pajamas

**5.**
Shape feet. Fold to back.

**6.**

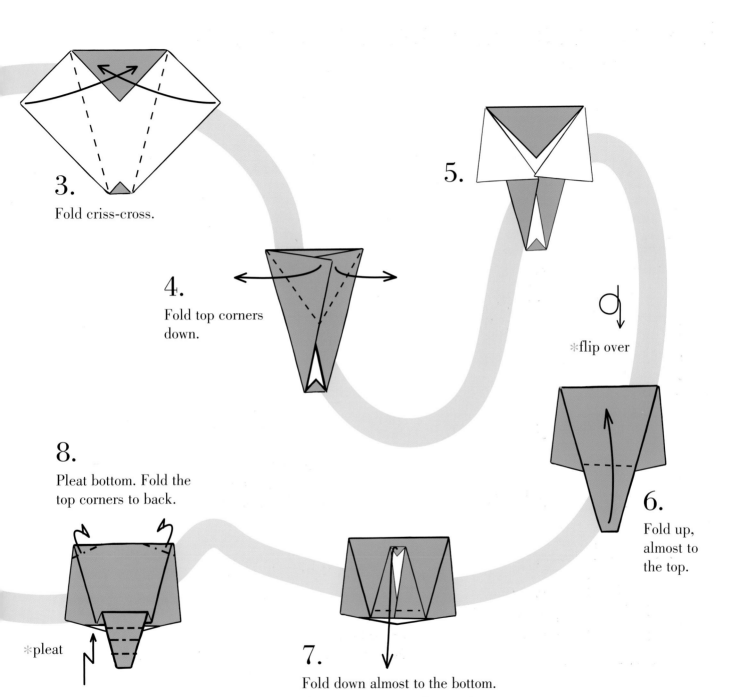

**3.**
Fold criss-cross.

**4.**
Fold top corners down.

**5.**

*flip over

**6.**
Fold up, almost to the top.

**7.**
Fold down almost to the bottom.

**8.**
Pleat bottom. Fold the top corners to back.

*pleat

# newspaper baseball mitt

This mitt is also good for picking up bugs!

◆◇◇◇ LEVEL OF DIFFICULTY

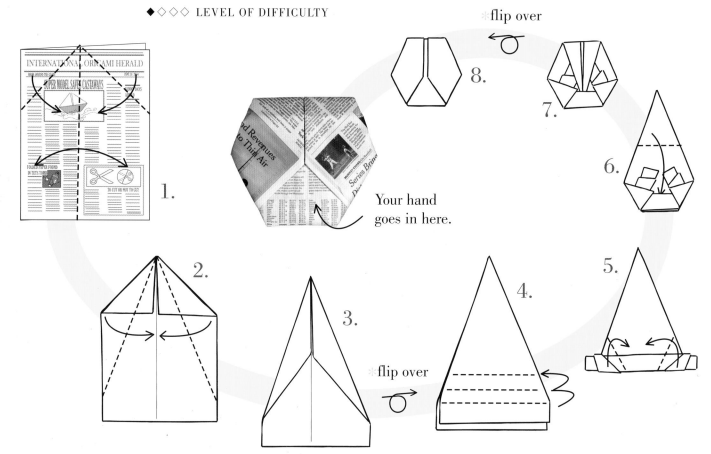

Your hand goes in here.

*flip over

*flip over

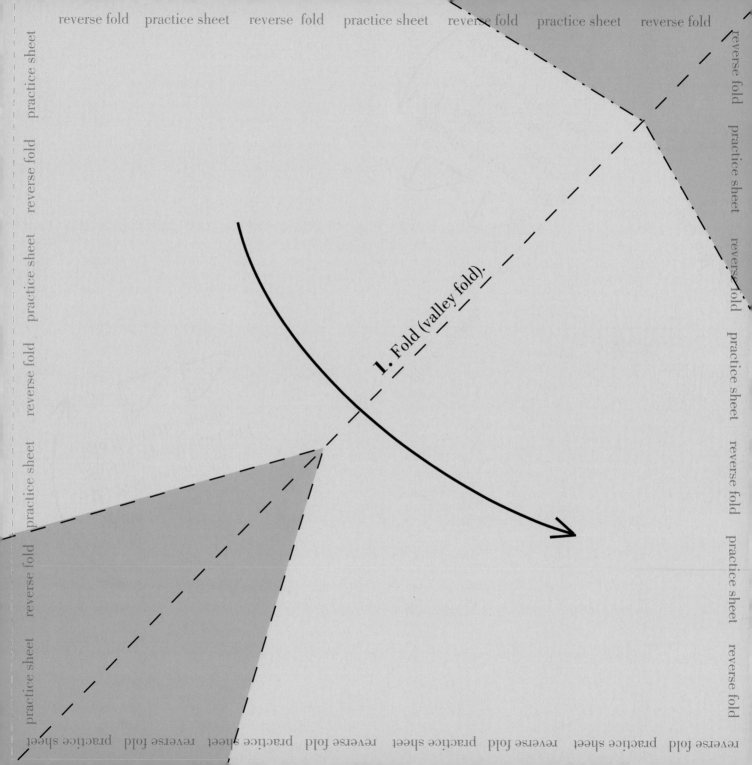

1. Fold (valley fold).

valley fold

mountain fold

**3.** Fold and unfold. Slightly open flap and fold to the outside of the model.

Outside Reverse Fold

**2.** Fold and unfold. Slightly open model and fold flap to the inside.

Inside Reverse Fold

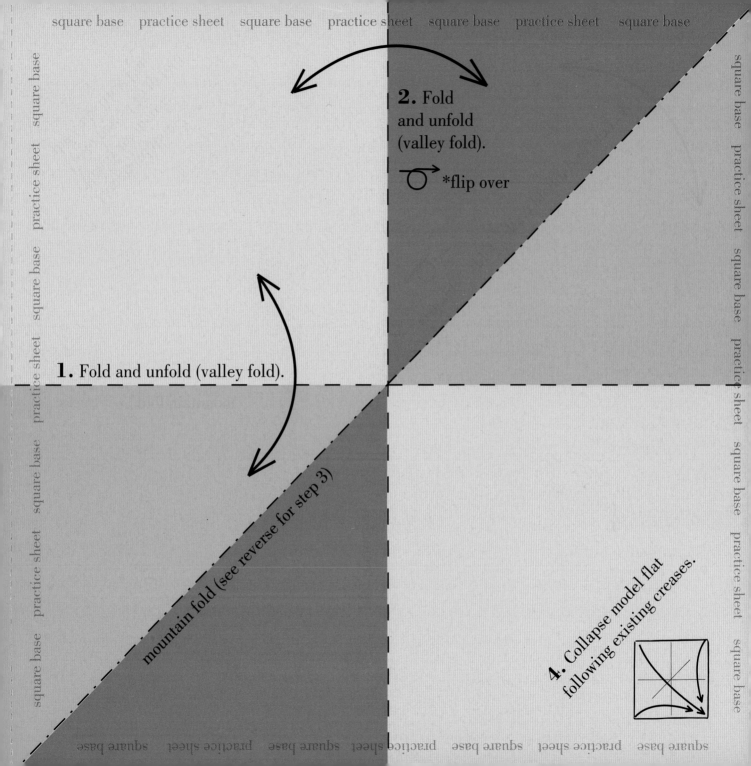

square base    practice sheet    square base    practice sheet    square base    practice sheet    square base

**2.** Fold
and unfold
(valley fold).

*flip over

**1.** Fold and unfold (valley fold).

mountain fold (see reverse for step 3)

**4.** Collapse model flat
following existing creases.

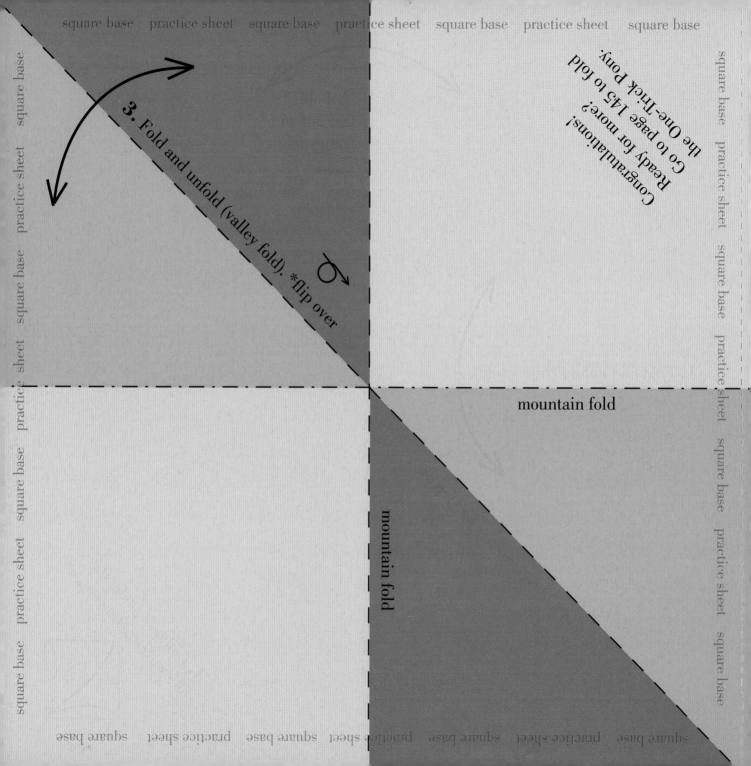

3. Fold and unfold (valley fold). *flip over

mountain fold

mountain fold

Congratulations!
Ready for more?
Go to page 145 to fold
the One-Trick Pony.

square base  practice sheet  square base  practice sheet  square base  practice sheet  square base

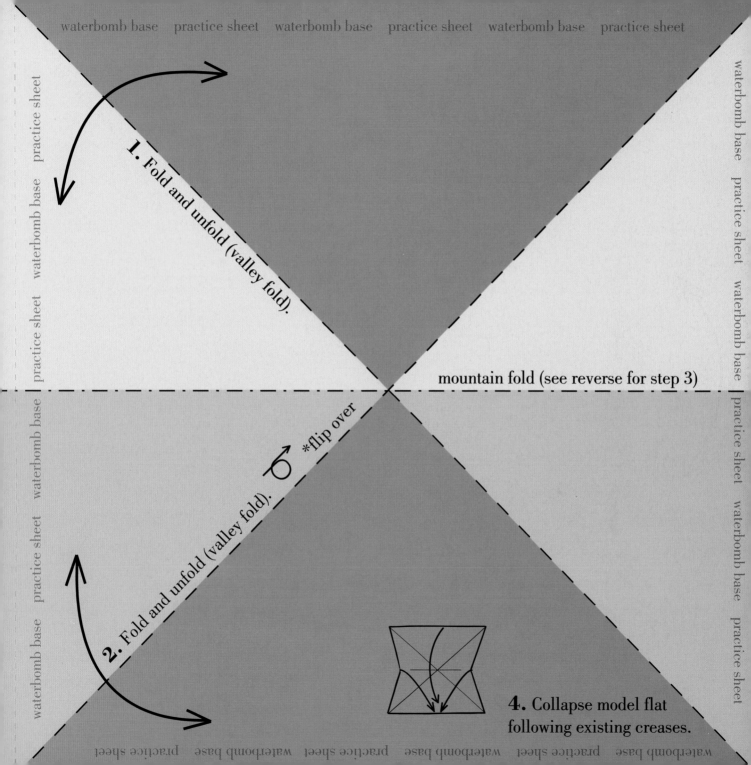

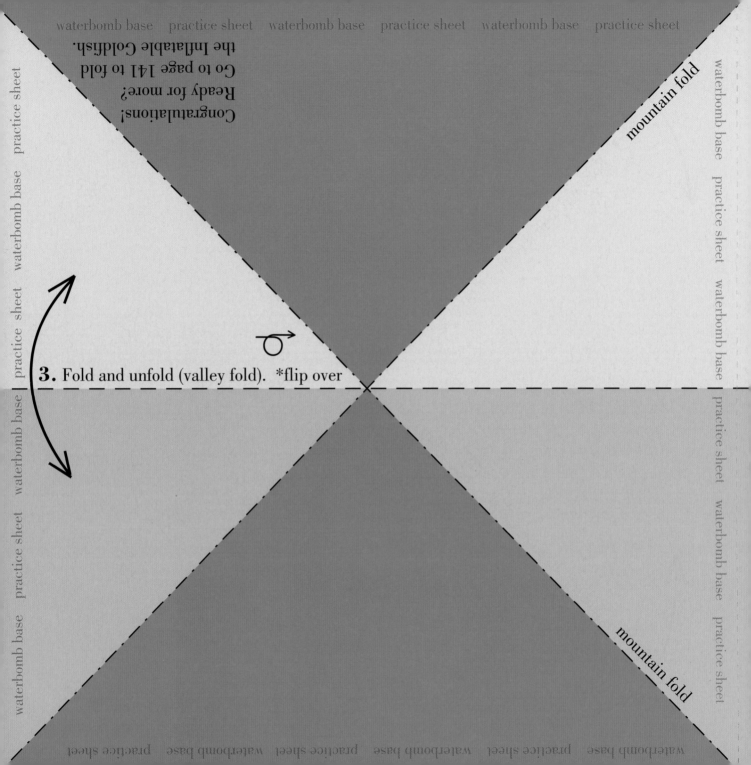

**3.** Fold and unfold (valley fold). *flip over

Congratulations!
Ready for more? Go to page 141 to fold
the Inflatable Goldfish.

mountain fold

mountain fold

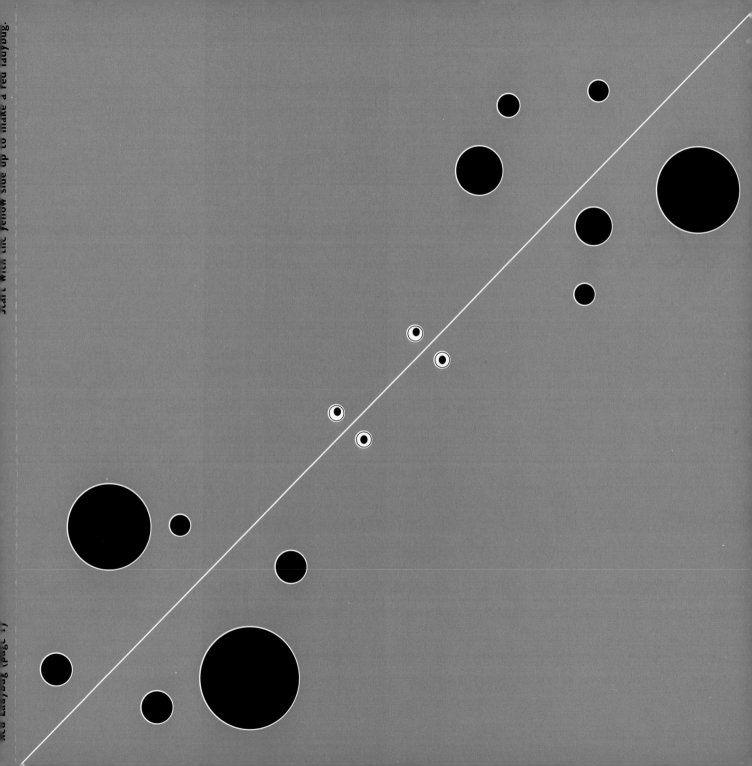

Start with the yellow side up to make a red ladybug.

Red Ladybug (page 1)

California Sunshine Ladybug (page 1)

Start with the red side up to make a yellow ladybug.

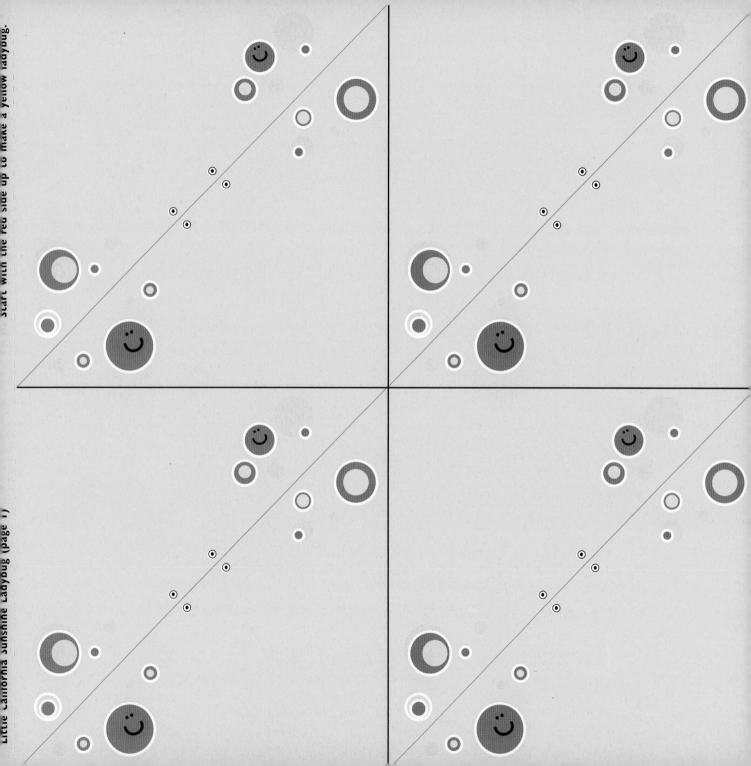

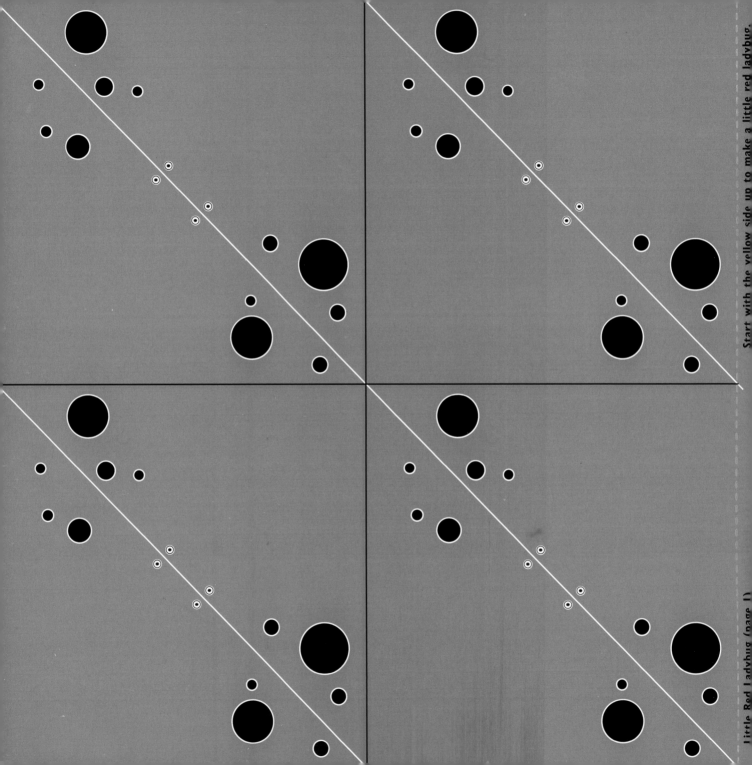

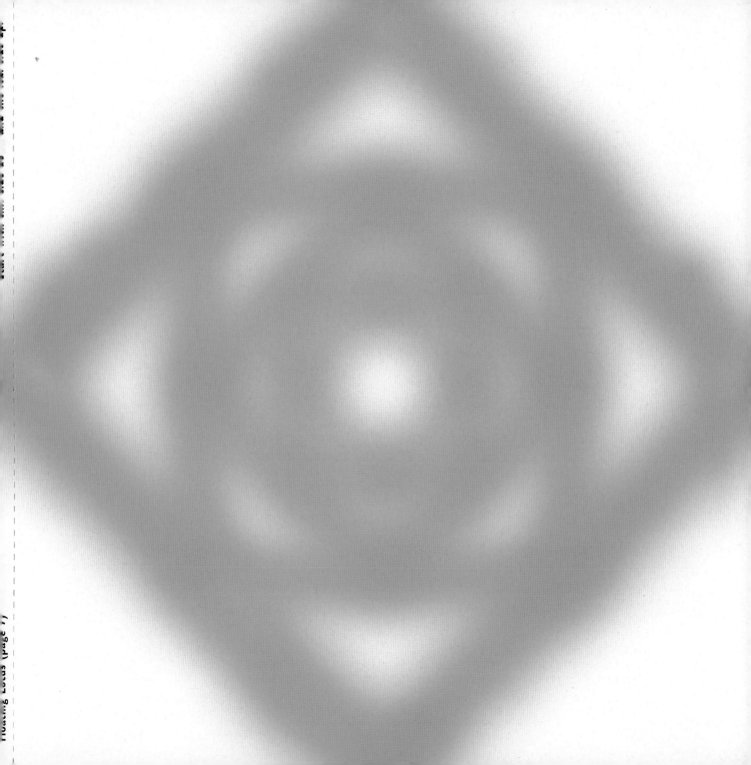

stems (page 14)

Start with this side down.

Spring Iris (page 15)

Cut into quarters. Mix or match 8 squares to make a Marigold.

Modular Marigold (page 19)

Cut into quarters. Mix or match 8 squares to make a Marigold.

Modular Marigold (page 19)

Modular Marigold (page 19)

Cut into quarters. Mix or match 8 squares to make a Marigold

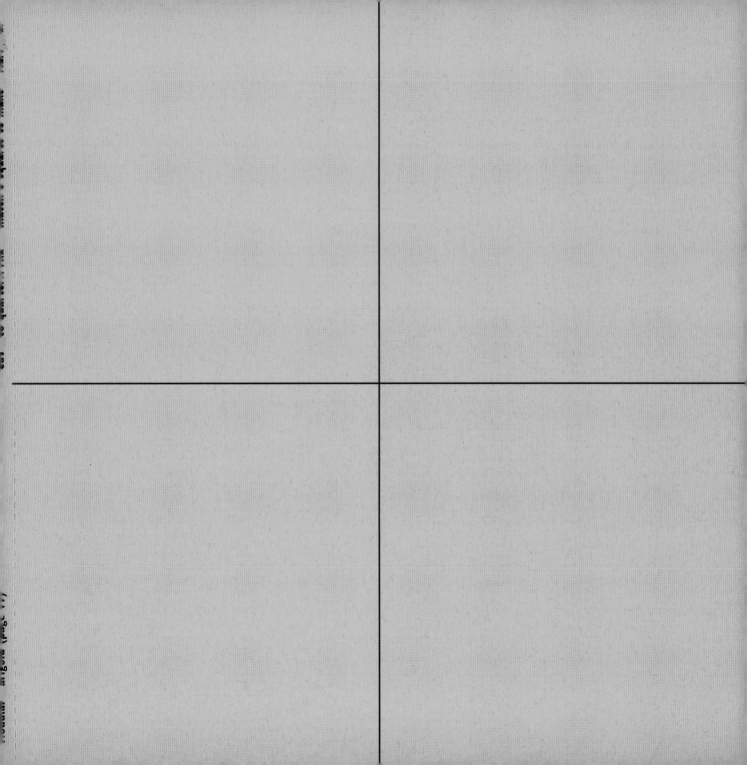

black & maple swan (page 23)

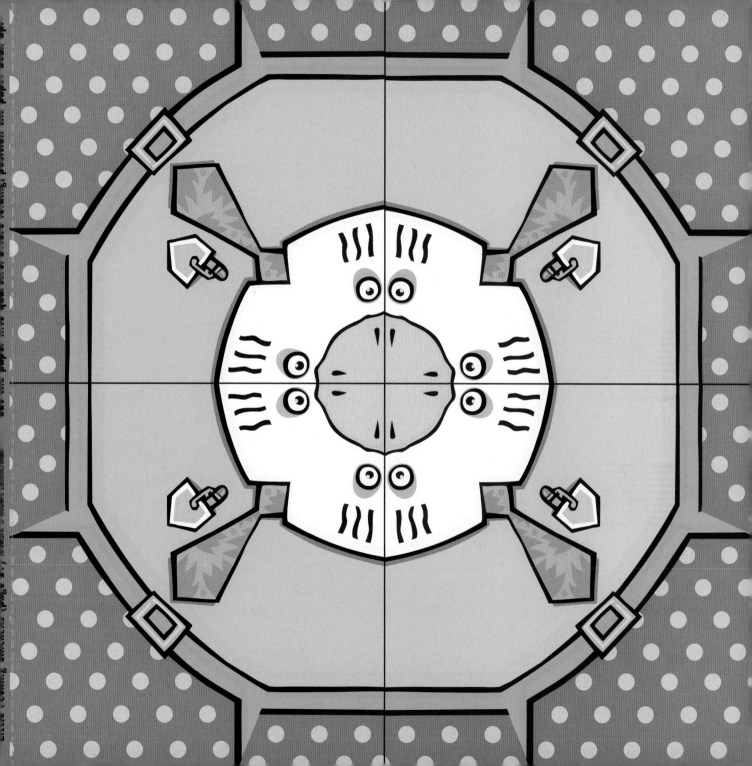

blue spiral (rapping blue of happiness (page 5 )) Artwork © Tom Rolofson | TrueTieDye.com

Cliff Swallow (page 39)

Before folding, position the paper so that the perforated edge is at the upper left.

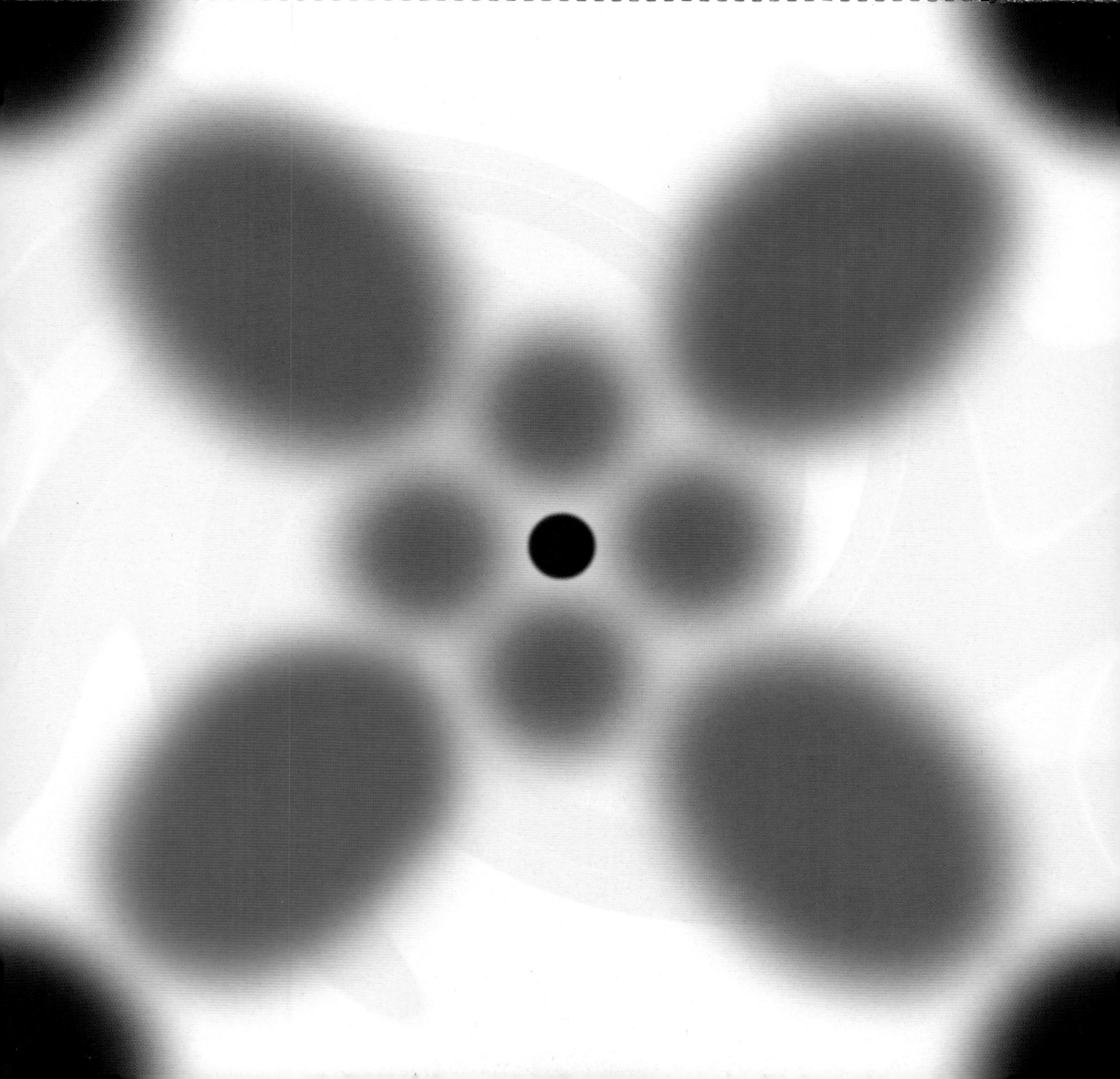

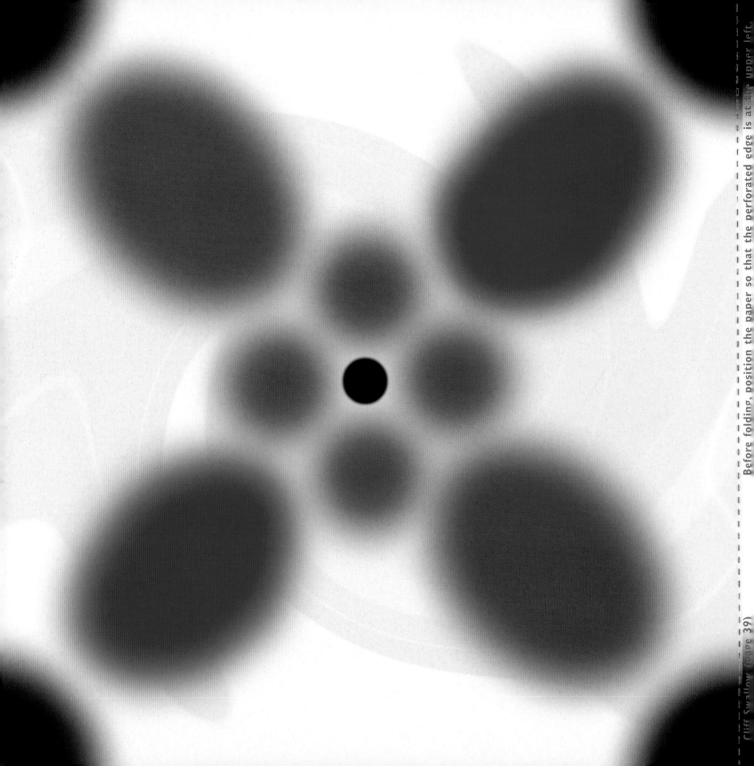

TOUCAN BEAK (page 47)

Before folding, position the paper so that the perforated edge is at the upper left

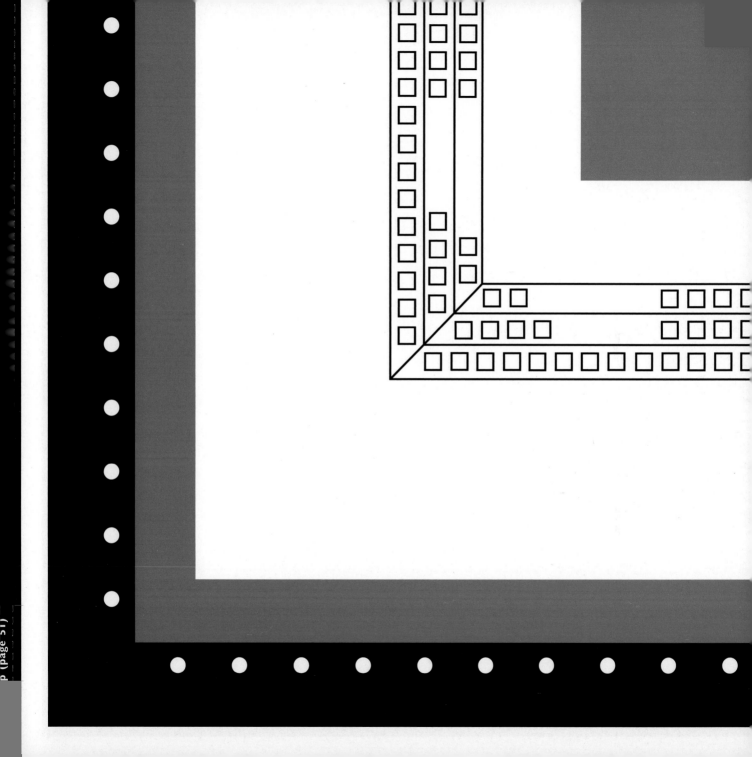

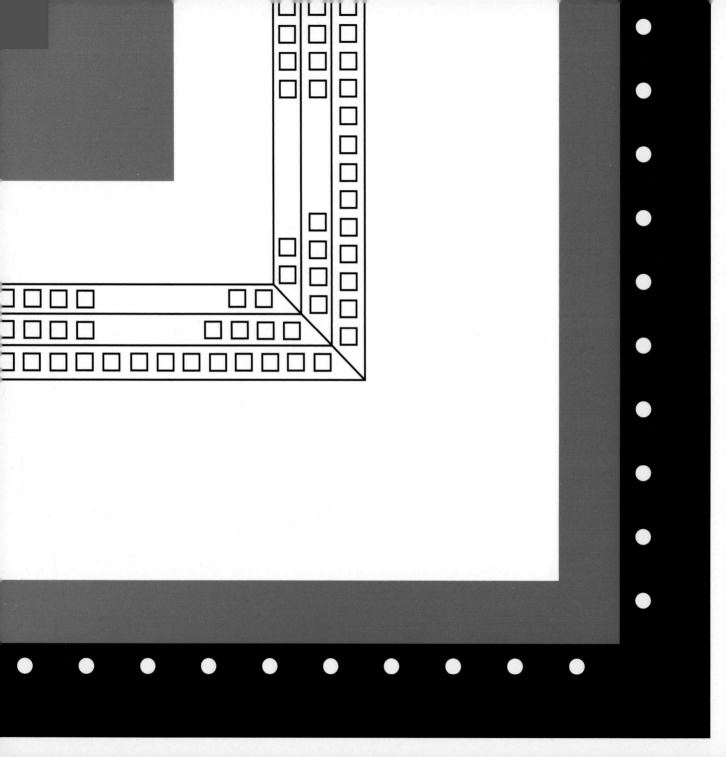

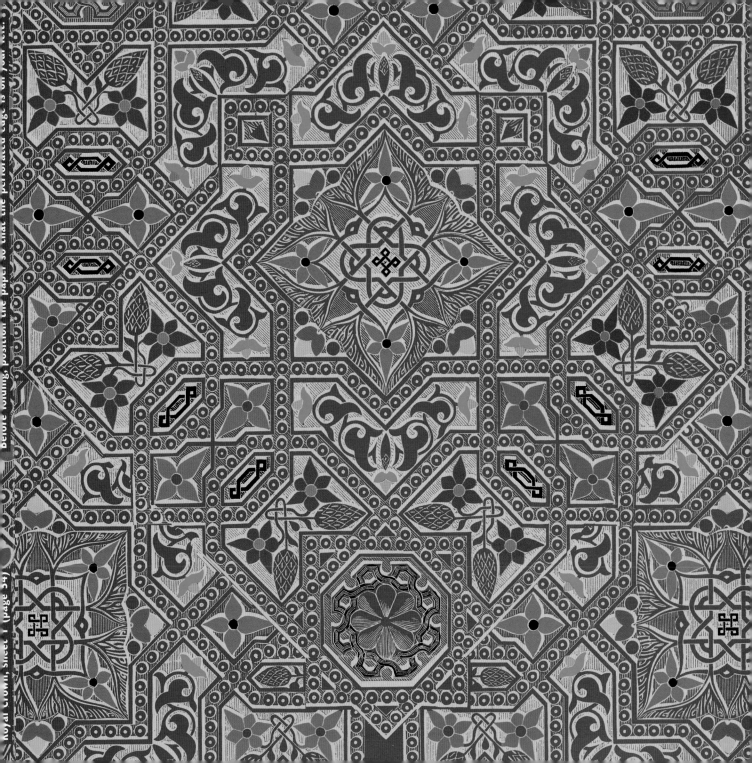

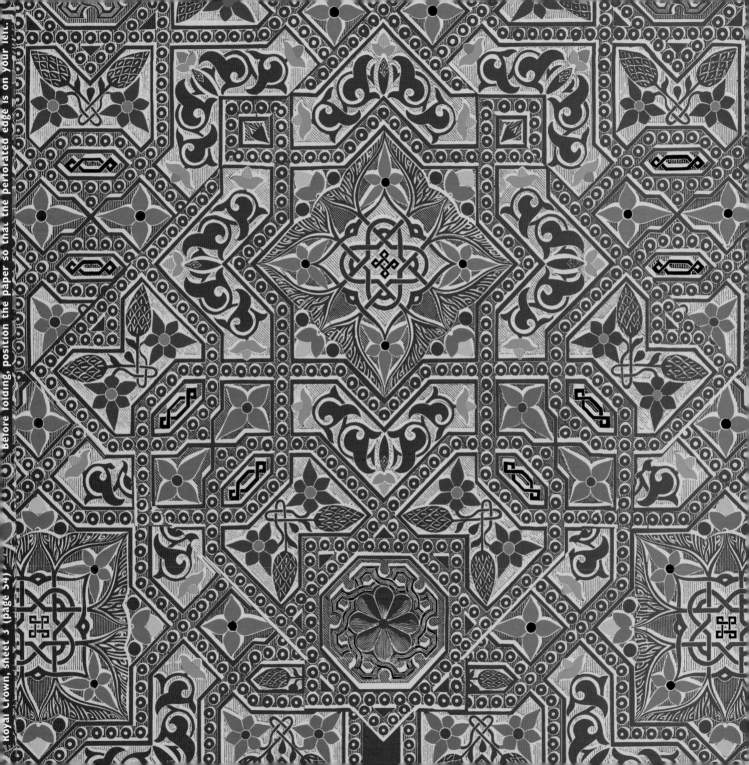

Before folding, position the paper so that the perforated edge is on your left.

Before folding, position the paper so that the perforated edge is on your left.

Before folding, position the paper so that the perforated edge is on your left.

Start with this side do...

Szarl: Ship of 1,000 Cranes (page 55)

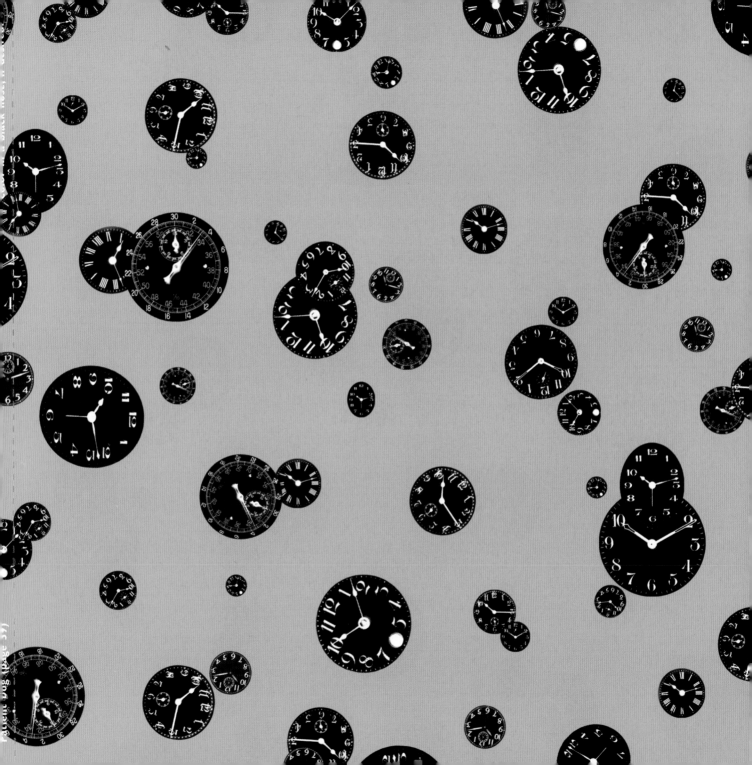

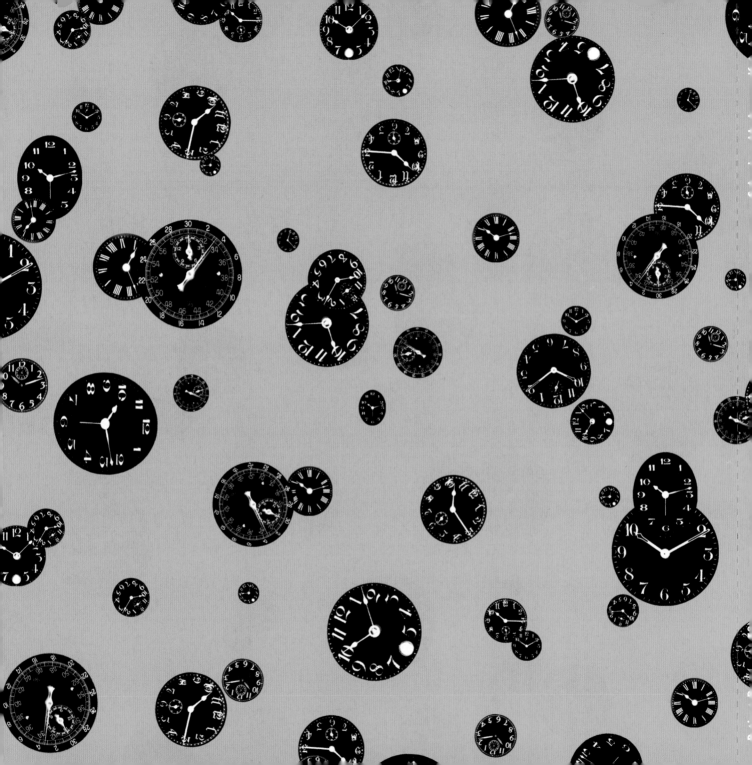

Dalmatian Patent Dog (page 57)

Dark Furry Cat (page 65)

Start with ___ is side up and the perforated edge on your left. Draw in eyes, if desired.

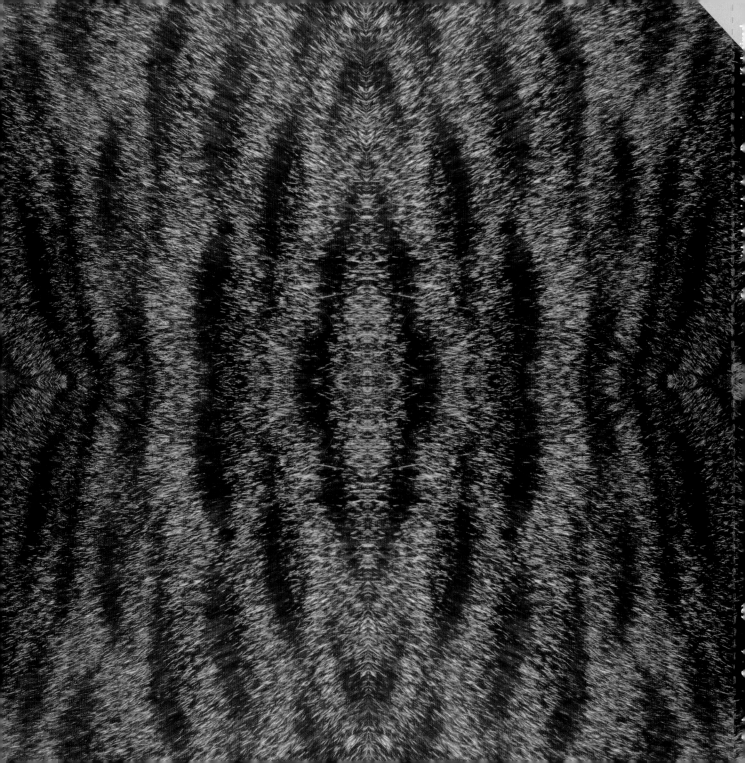

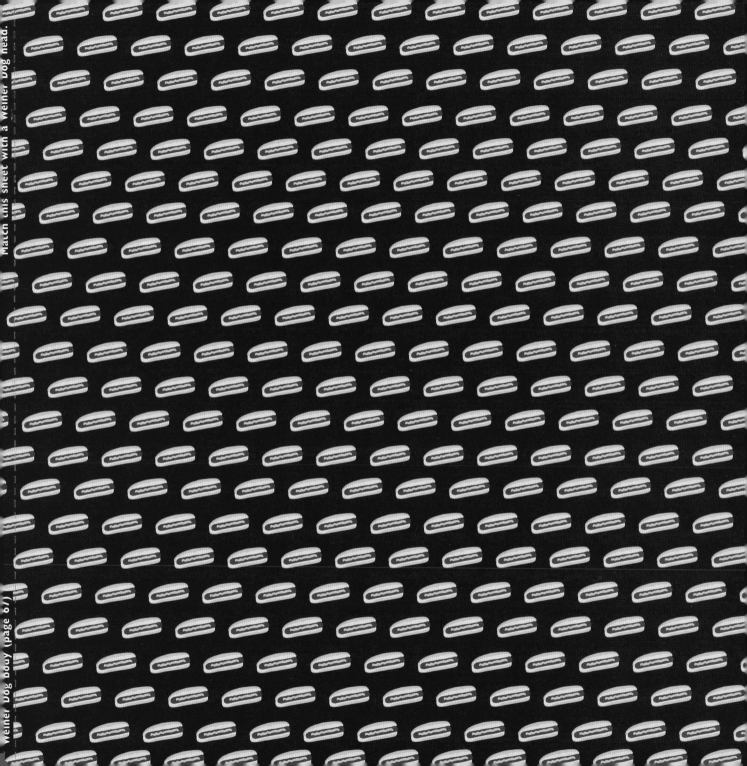

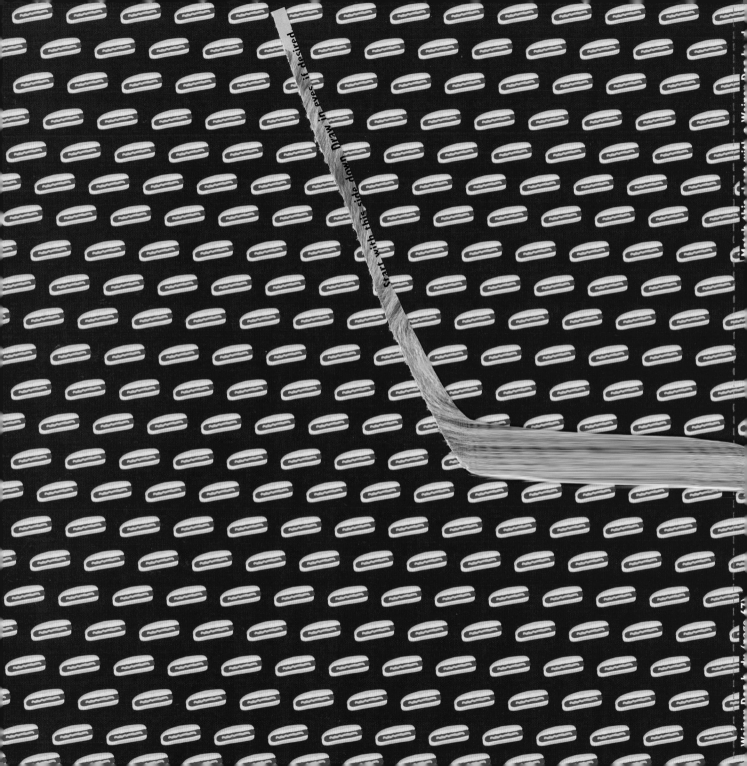

Weiner Dog head (page 67) Cut in half vertically. Before folding, position the paper so that the center black square is on your left.

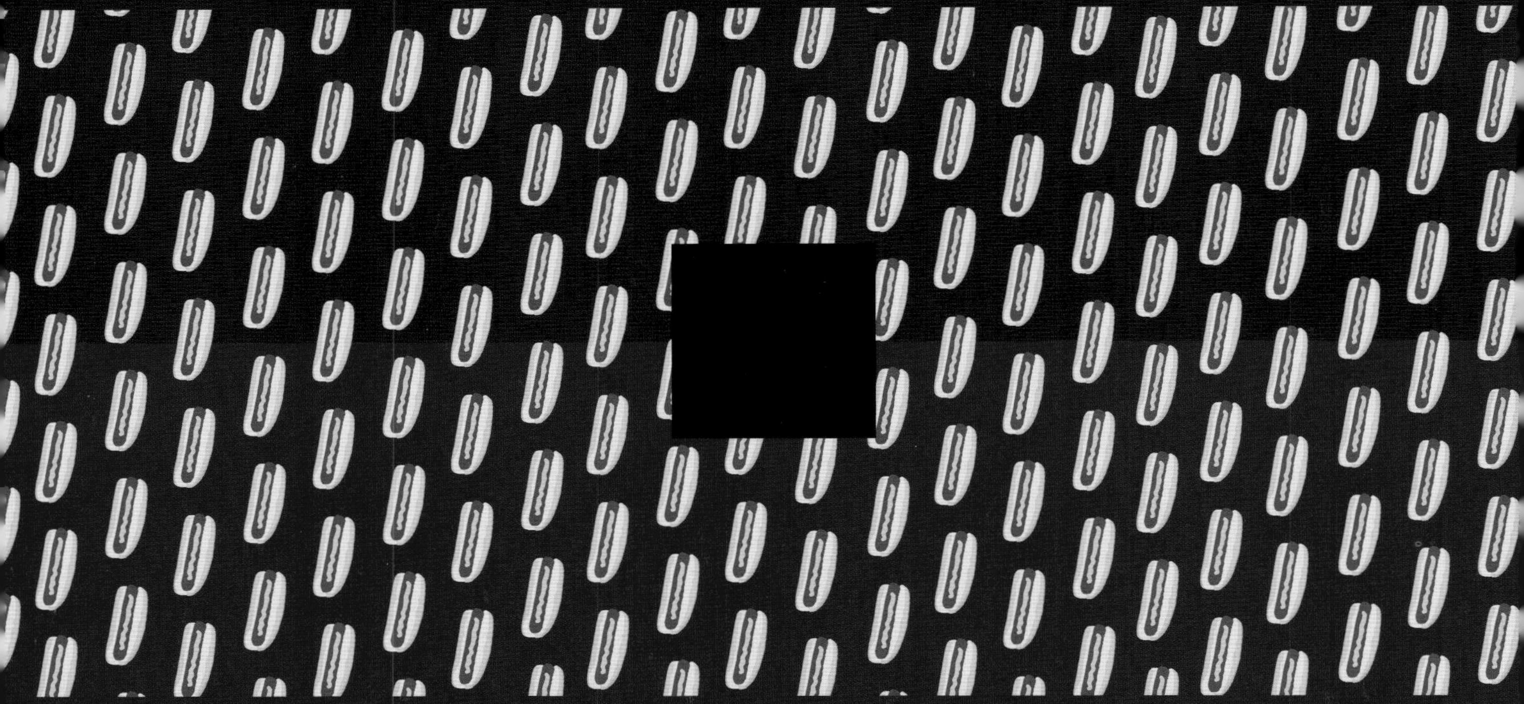

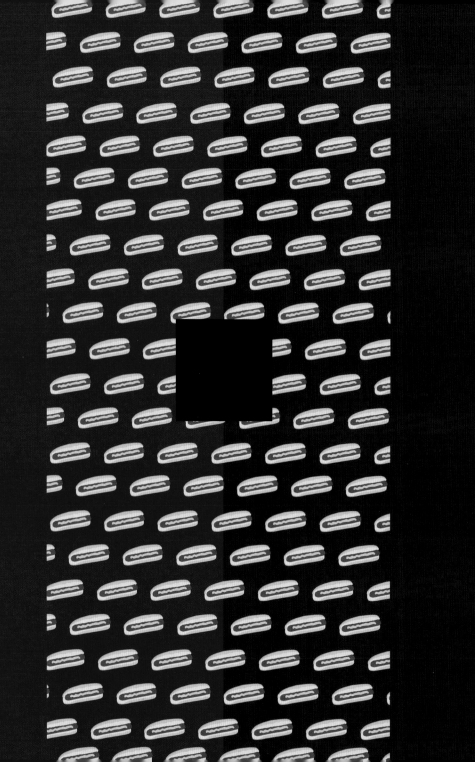

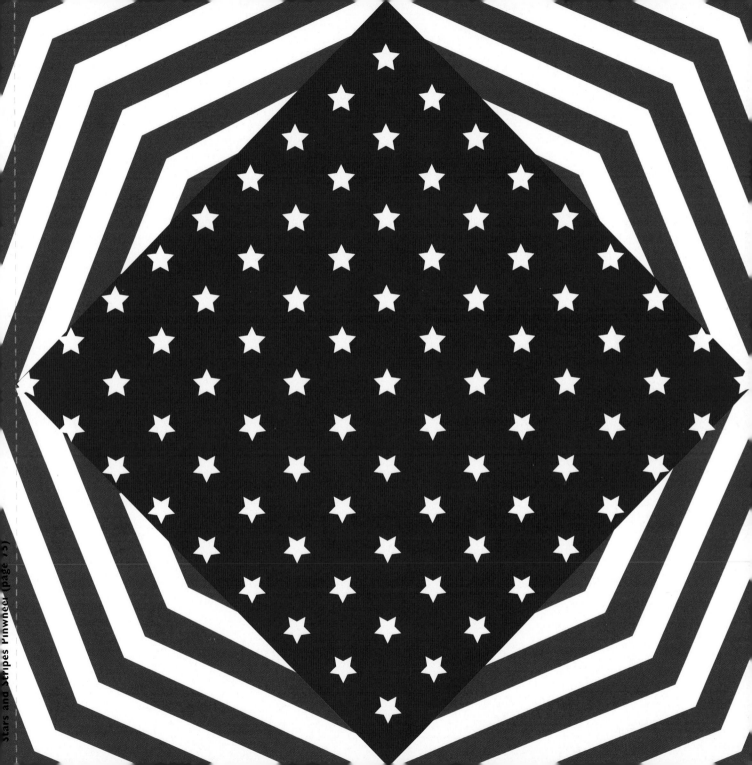

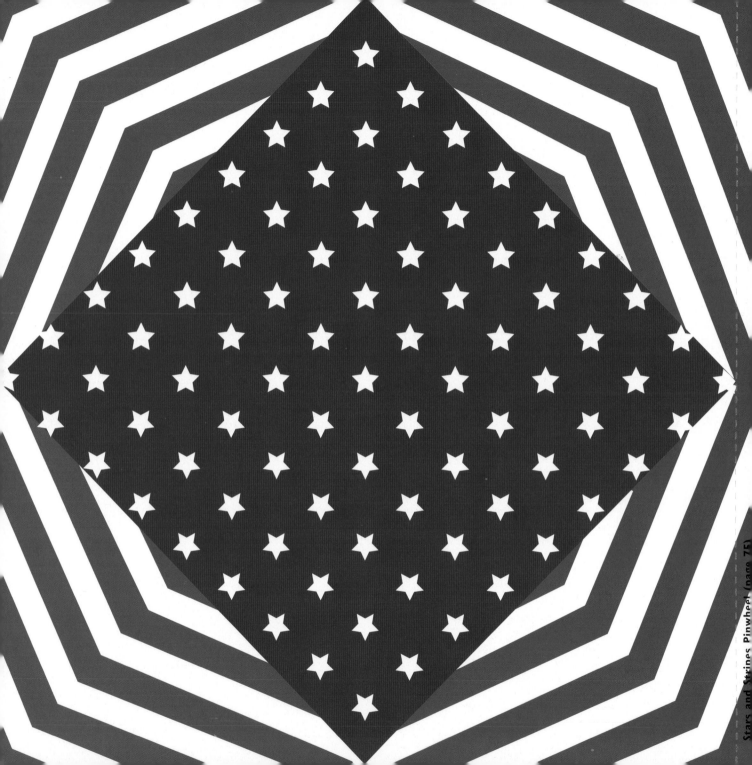

Stars and Stripes Pinwheel (page 75)

This is for the large basket. Cut the long strip from the Mini-Summer basket sheet for the handle.

Summer Basket (page 77)

ini-summer basket and handles (page 77) Cut out handles. Remaining paper is for a small basket (the short strip is its handle).

Mini-Summer Basket and handles (page 77). Cut out handles. Remaining paper is for a small basket (the short strip is its handle).

Hunter Green Leprechaun Hat (page 83)

Start folding with the perforated edge on your left and this side up.

Lime Green Leprechaun Hat (page 83)

Start folding with the perforated edge on your left and this side up.

Start wit this side down

Bamboo Pagoda Tower, sheet 2 (page 91)    Start with the bamboo side down.

Start with this side up.

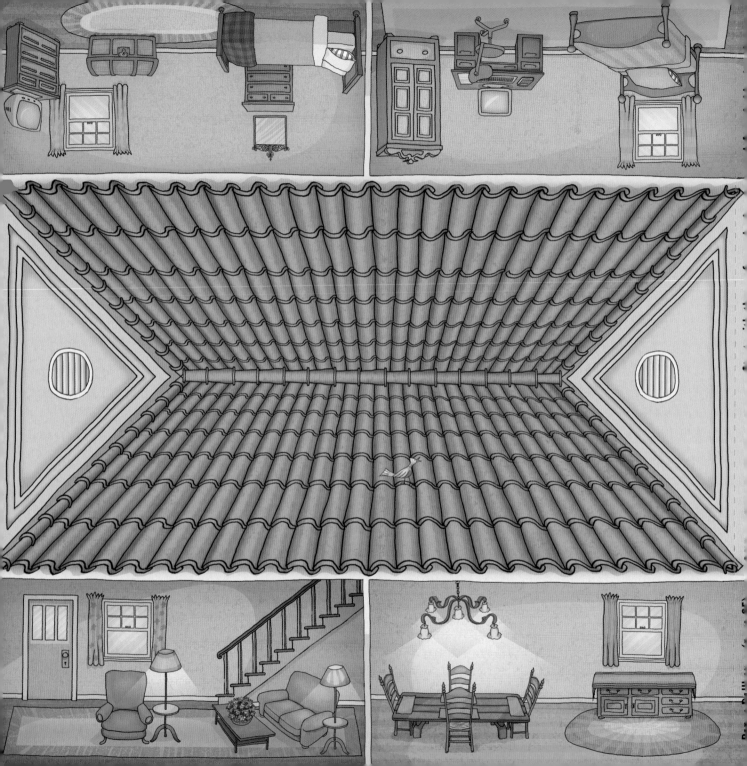

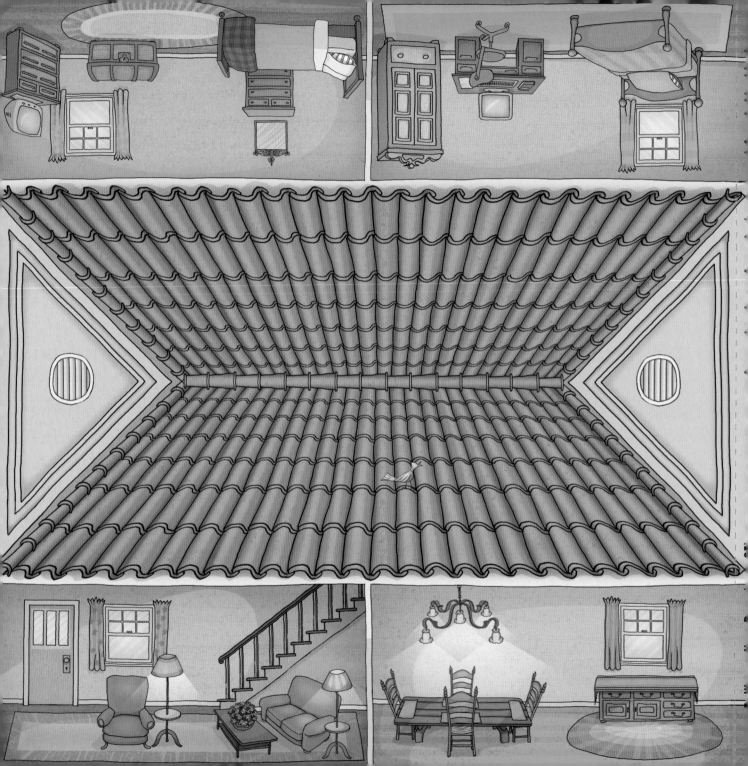

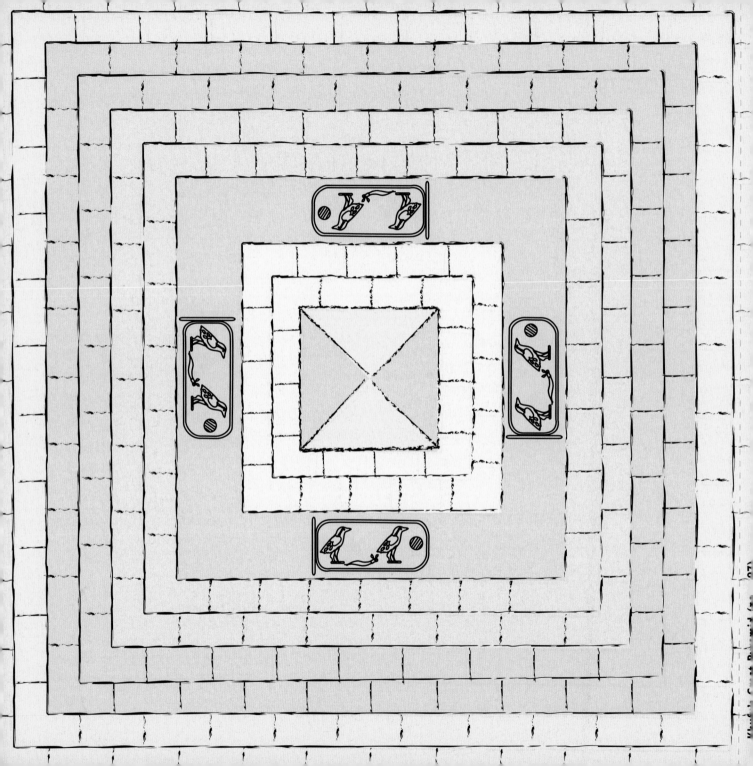

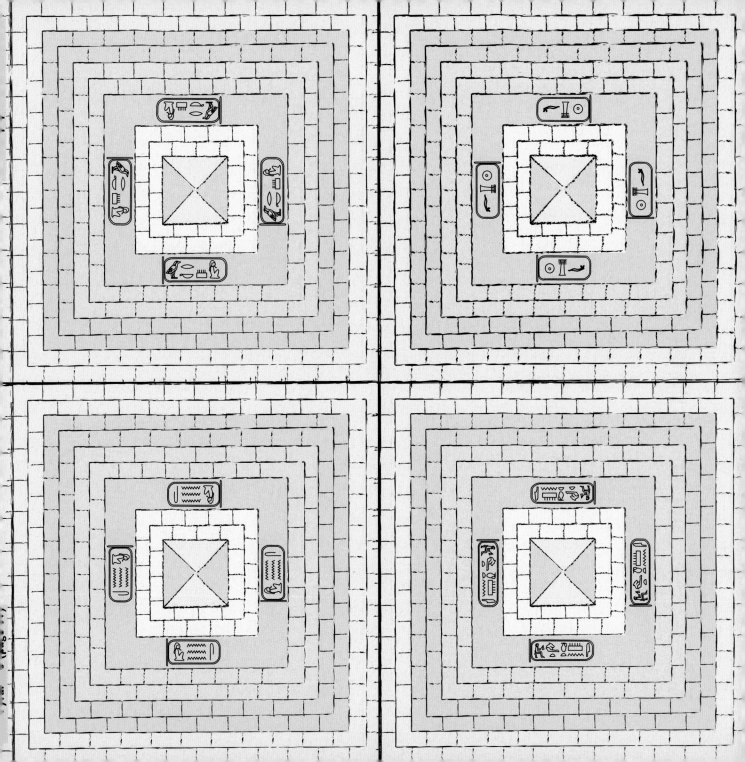

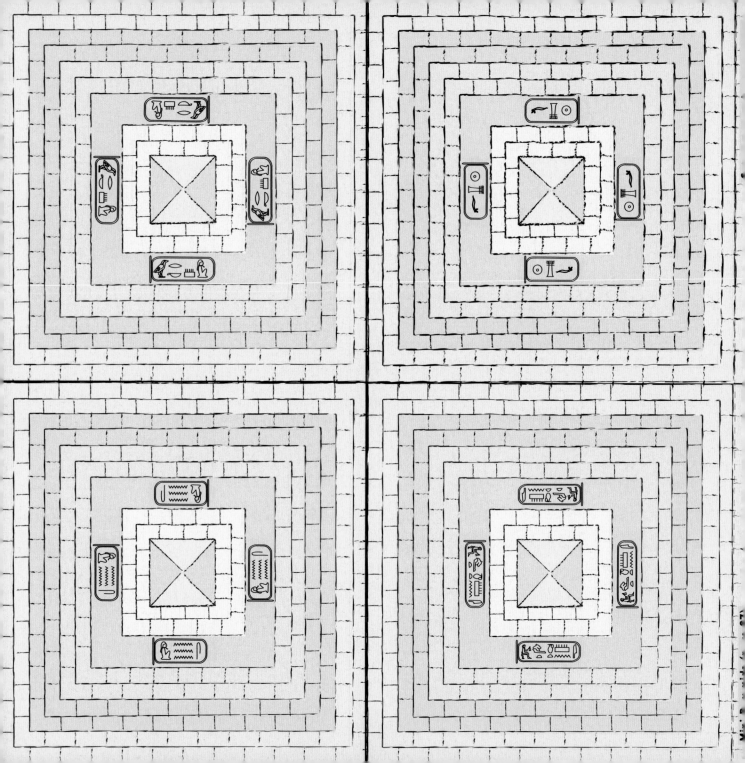

The Rabbit of Wisdom (page 105)

Position the paper so that the perforated edge is at the upper left.

Before folding, position the paper so that the perforated edge is at the upper left.

Oh, Lucky Day Good Luck Fish (page 101)

Before folding, position the paper so that the perforated edge is at the upper left.

Start with the perforated edge on your left.

Solar System Ninja Star (page 109)

Start with the perforated edge on your left.

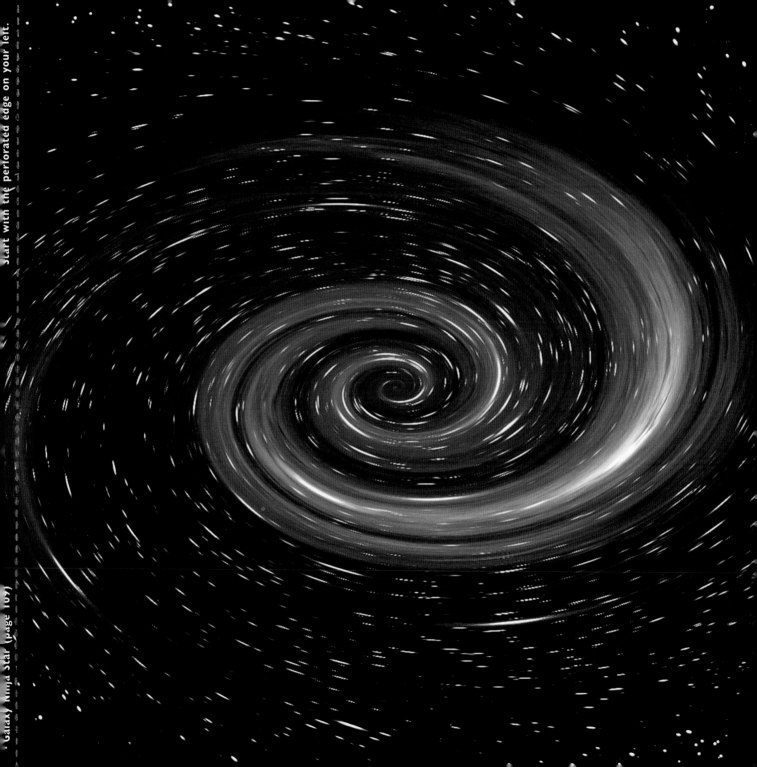

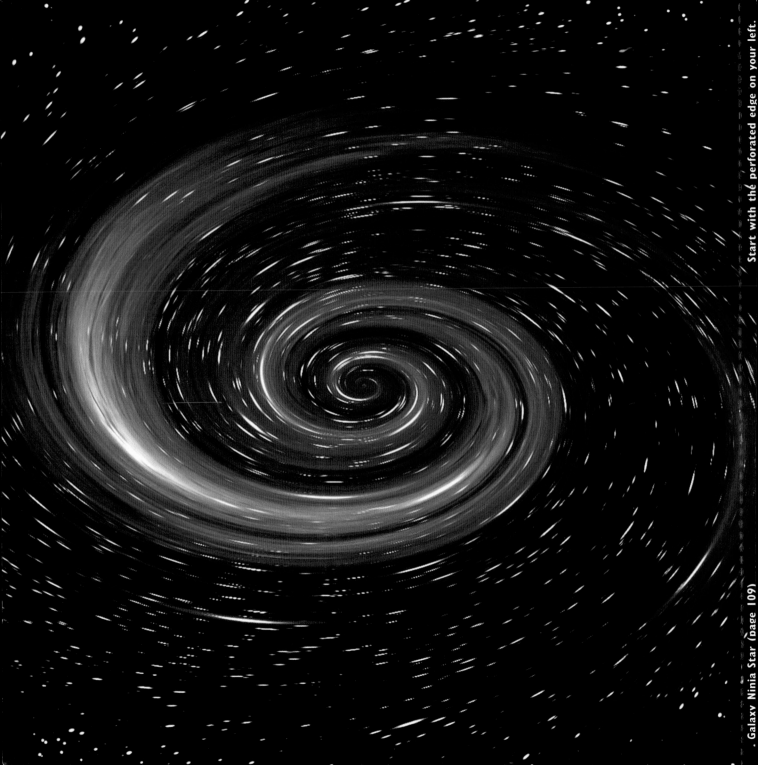

Start with the perforated edge on your left.

Galaxy Ninja Star (page 109)

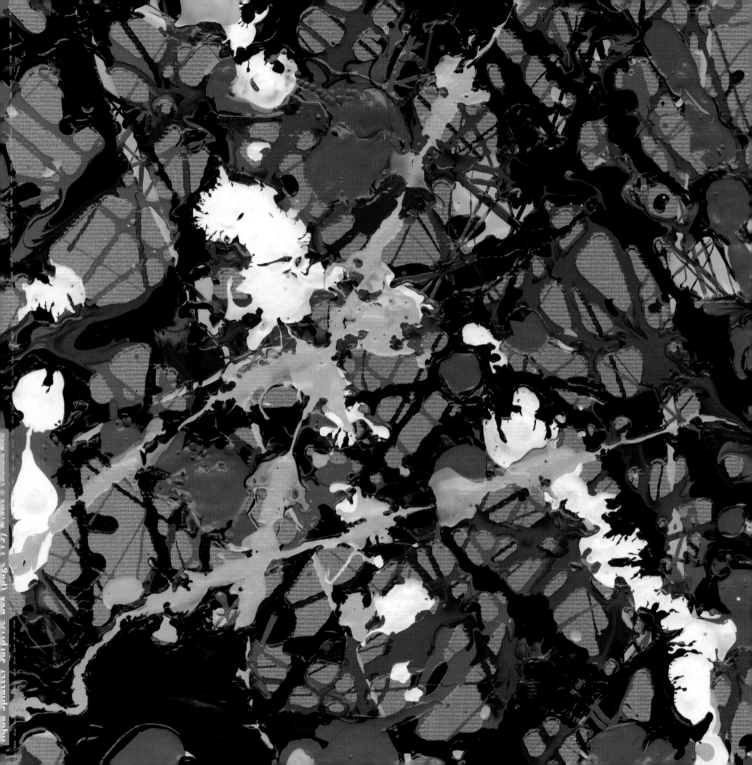

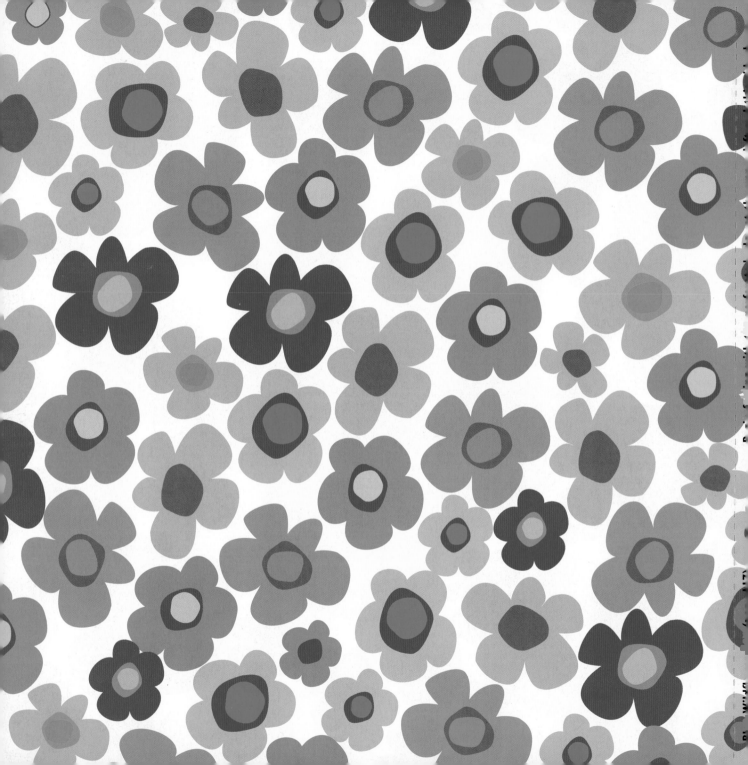

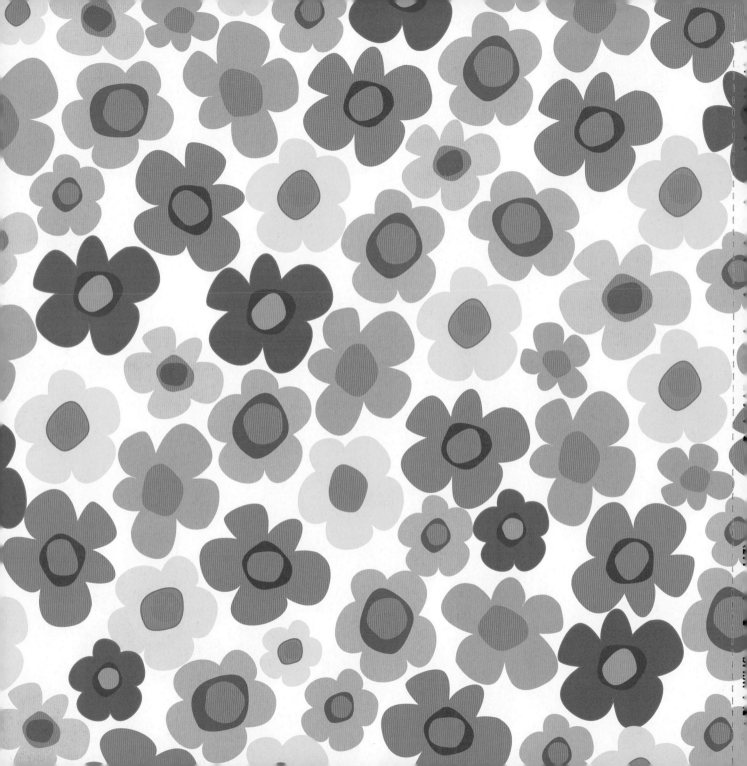

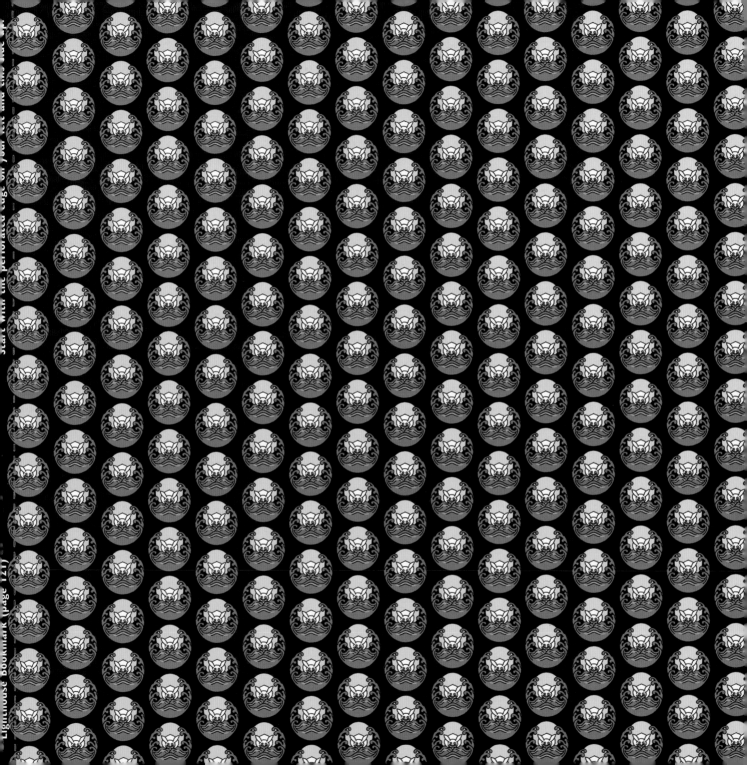

Start with the perforated edge on your left and this side down.

Lighthouse Bookmark (page 121)

Pop-Up Greeting Card interior (page 125)

Start with the perforated edge on your left and this side up.

Pop-Up Greeting Card Interior (page 125)

Start with the perforated edge on your left and this side down.

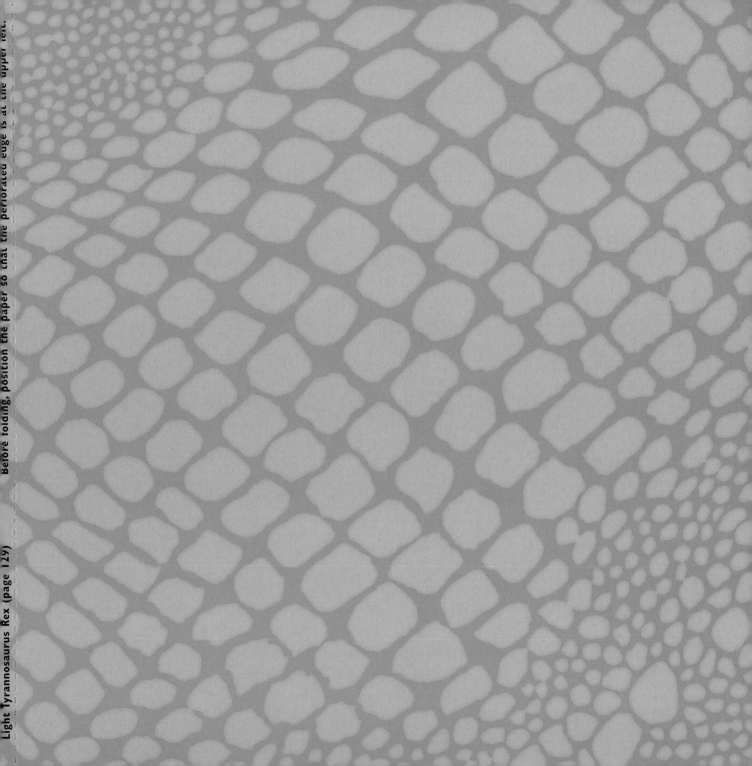

Before folding, position the paper so that the perforated edge is at the upper left.

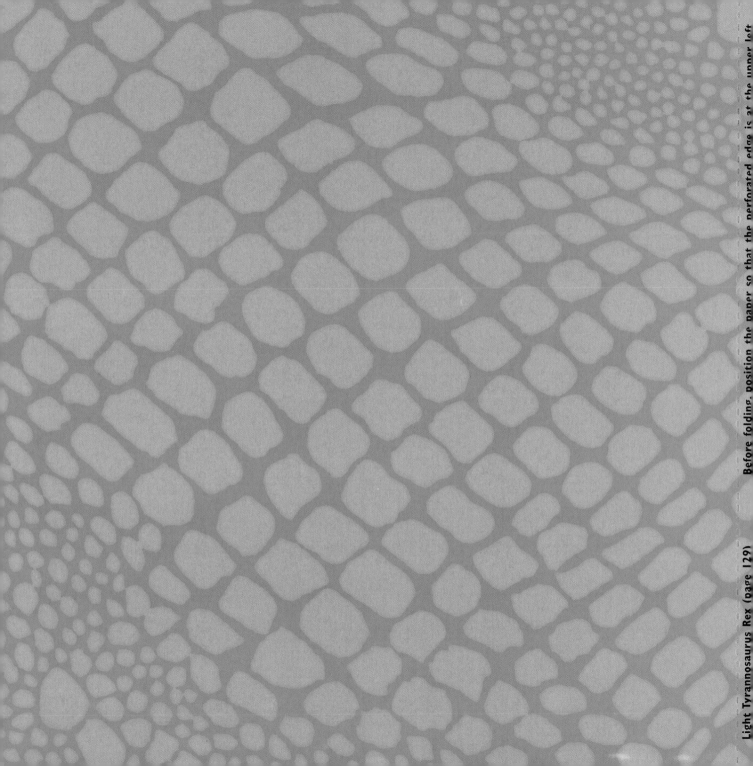

Before folding, position the paper so that the perforated edge is at the upper left.

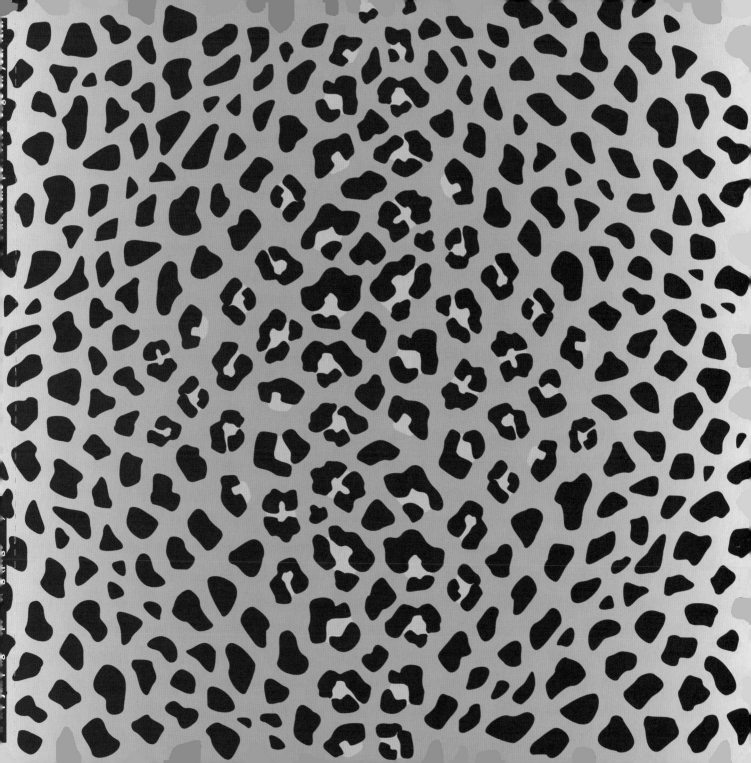

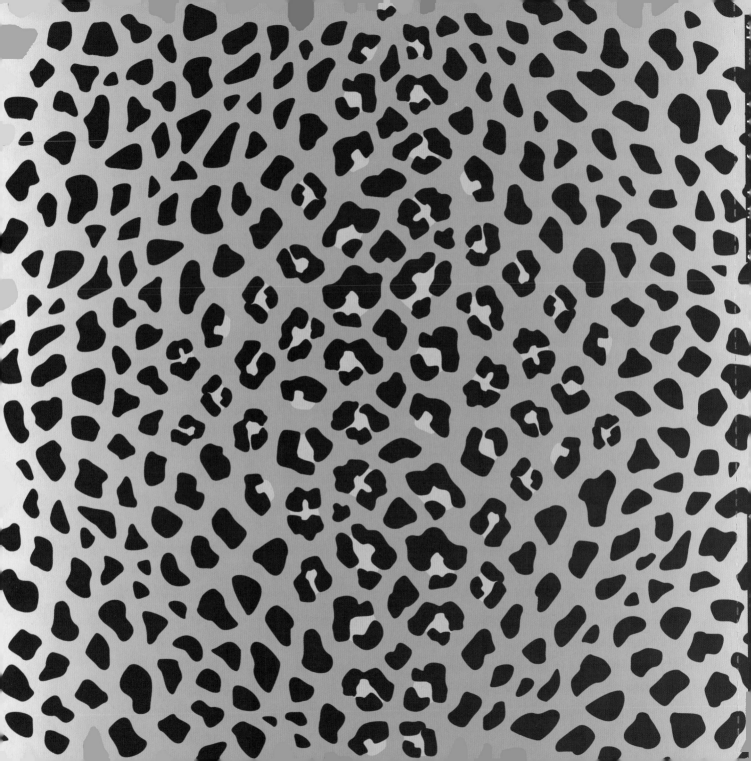

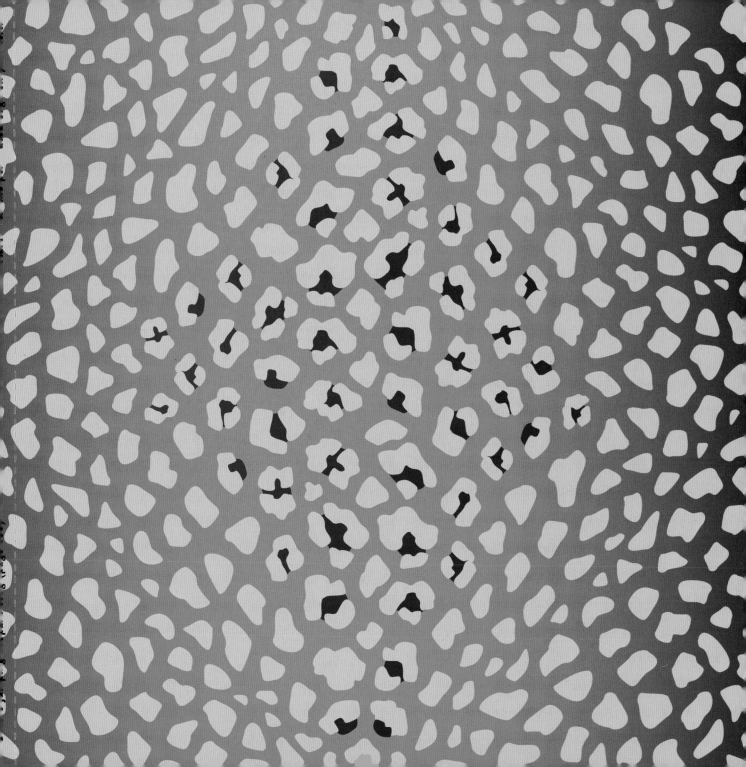

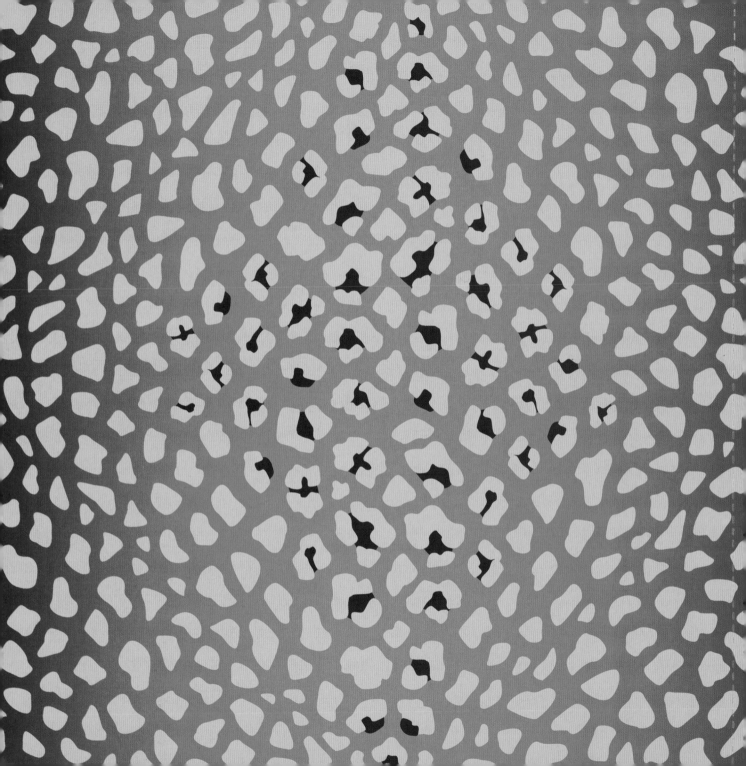

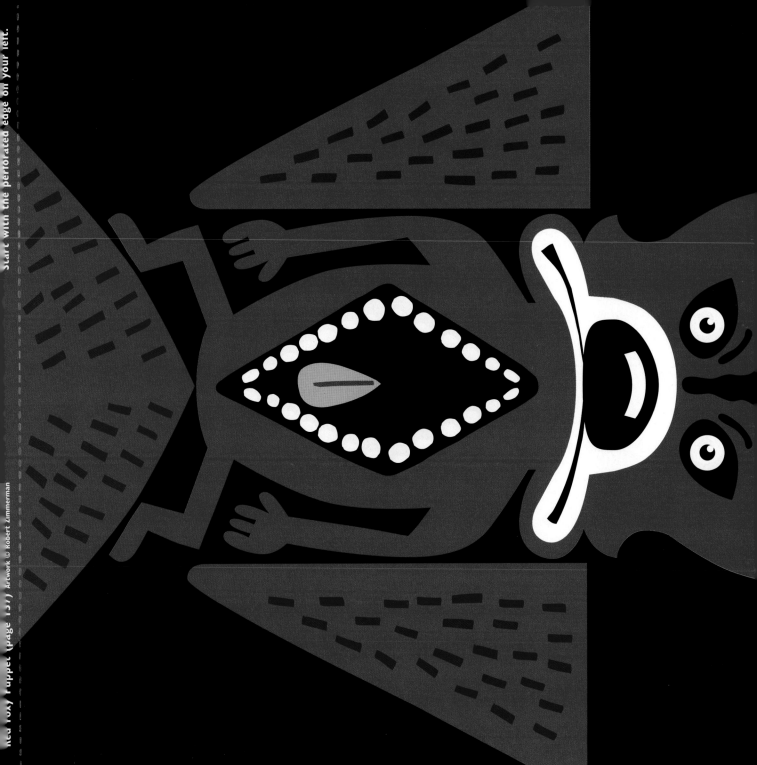

Red Foxy Puppet (page 131) Artwork © Robert Zimmerman          Start with the perforated edge on your left.

Start with the perforated edge on your left.

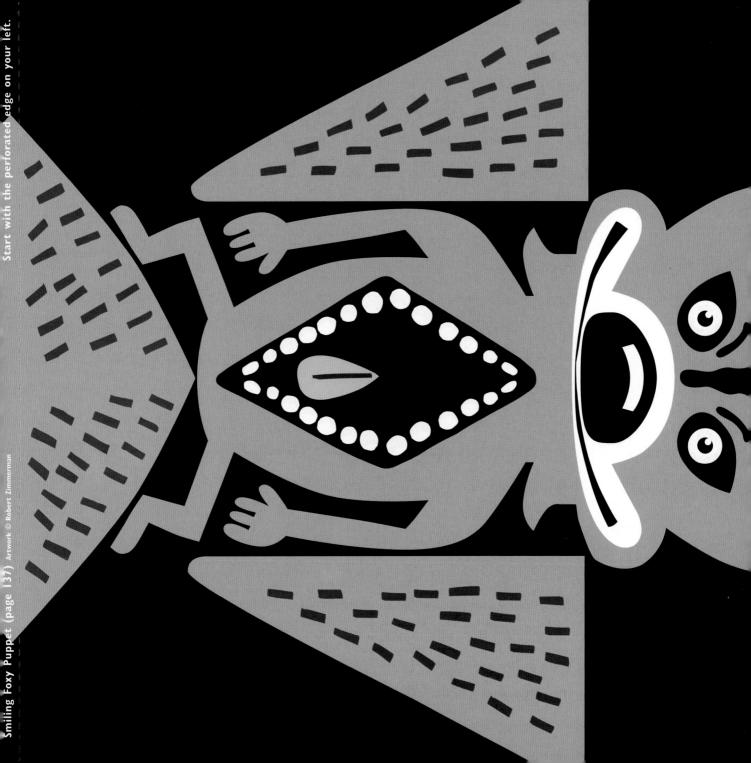

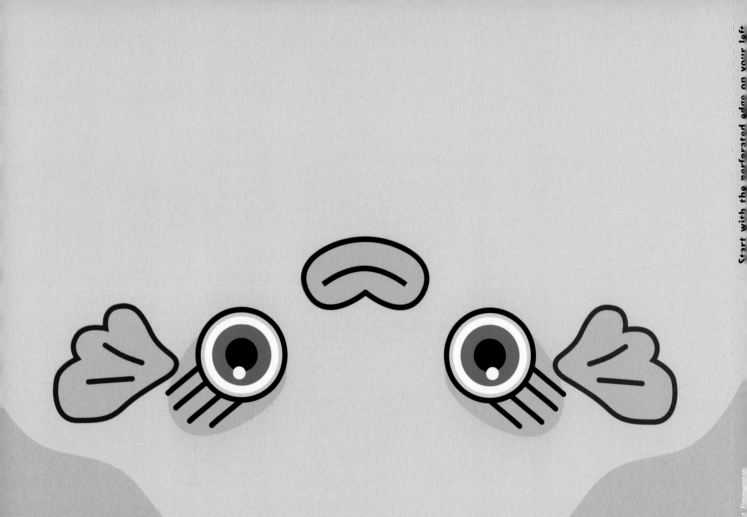

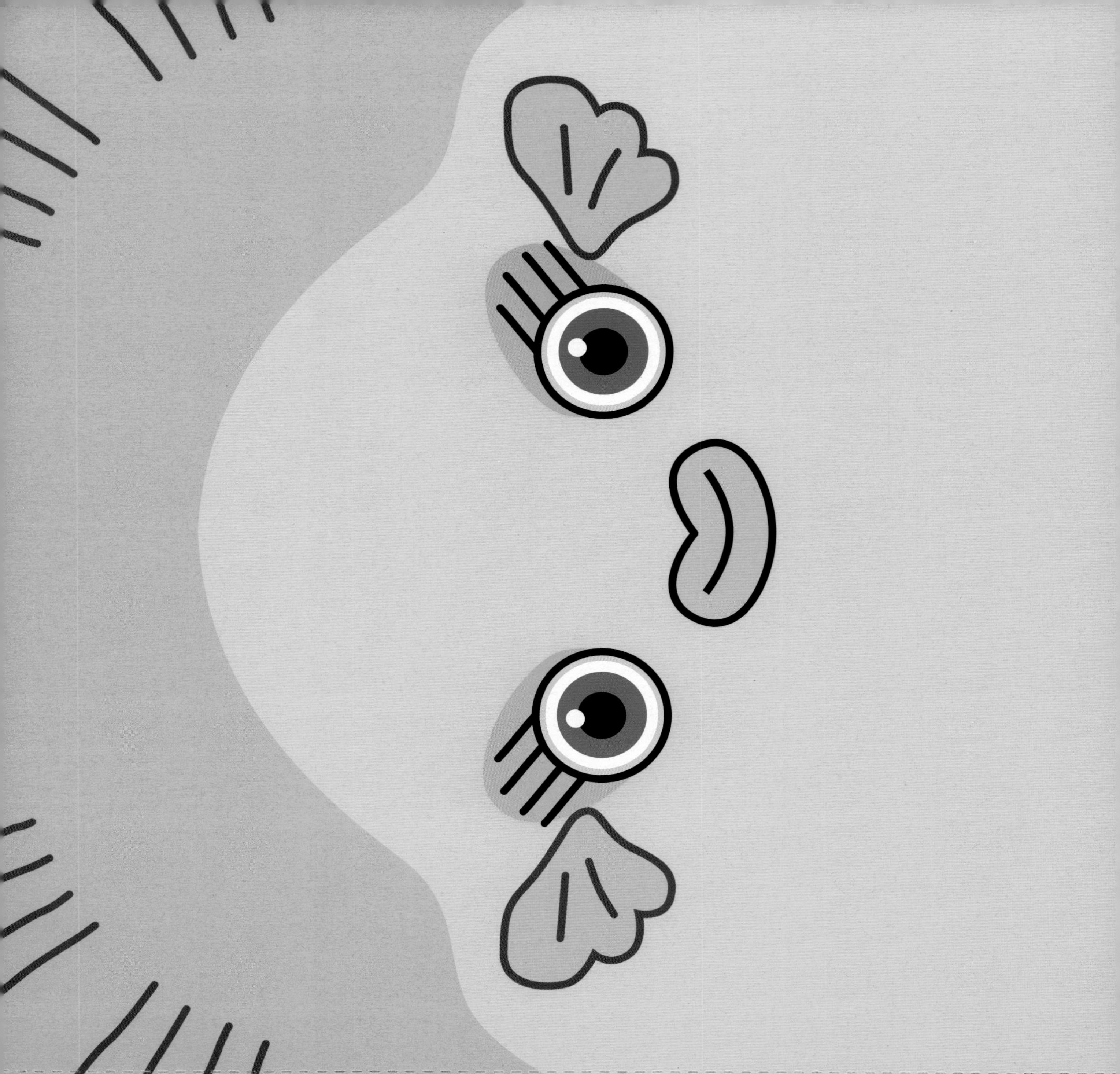

Inflatable Goldfish (page 141) 

Start with the perforated edge on your left.

Classic PJs or Elephant-In Pajamas (page 147).

Start with the perforated edge on your left and this side down.

Classic PJs for Elephant in Pajamas (page 149)

Elephant's head for Elephant in Pajamas (page 149)

Draw on eyes if desired

*E*

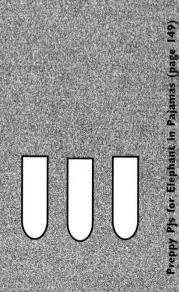

Start with the perforated edge on your left and this side down.

Elephant's head for Elephant in Pajamas (page 149)

Draw on eyes if desired.

Draw on eyes if desired